A Great and Good Man

RARE, FIRST-HAND ACCOUNTS AND OBSERVATIONS OF ABRAHAM LINCOLN

EDITED BY JONATHAN W. WHITE AND WILLIAM J. GRIFFING
FOREWORD BY WALTER STAHR

Reedy Press
PO Box 5131
St. Louis, MO 63139, USA
reedypress.com

Library of Congress Control Number: 2024946655

ISBN: 9781681065458

Printed in the United States of America

26 27 28 5 4 3 2

Contents

Foreword

by Walter Stahr

Writing a history book is like building a castle with a child's plastic bricks. The castle that you can create is limited by the bricks that you have on hand. There are of course many bricks already available for writing a life of Abraham Lincoln or a history of the Civil War. There are letters and diaries and newspapers and memoirs. But what this wonderful little book highlights is that there are yet more bricks out there, waiting to be discovered in attics and basements, waiting to be transcribed and published. This book is a colorful collection of new bricks, which will enable us to build new and better castles—in other words, to write new and better accounts of Lincoln and the Civil War.

The letters and diary entries presented here are especially interesting, for me, because they are almost all *contemporary* primary sources. There has been far too much tendency, in my view, in writing the life of Lincoln, to rely upon memoirs, often written decades after Lincoln's death. To take one obvious example, almost everybody "knows" that immediately after Lincoln's death, his secretary of war, Edwin Stanton, said "now he belongs to the ages." (Some people contend that Stanton said "now he belongs to the angels.") But neither version of Stanton's quote appeared in the newspapers—

which printed detailed accounts of Lincoln's death—in April 1865, nor in letters written in that month by those present at his death. No, the source of the famous quotation is an 1890 article by Lincoln's secretaries, John Hay and John Nicolay. I believe, based on the contemporary sources, that Stanton probably did not say *anything* right after Lincoln died.

I have written four biographies of American leaders, including three about members of the Lincoln cabinet: William Seward, Edwin Stanton, and Salmon Chase. I wish that this book had been in print when I wrote those books, because there are quotes here that I would have loved to include in my biographies.

I hope that this book will not only inspire castle-builders to use these new bricks in writing new books about Lincoln, his cabinet, and the Civil War. I hope this book will also inspire people to search through their attics and basements, or to encourage friends and neighbors to make such searches, for long-lost letters and diaries. The process of gathering sources, and writing history, is not completed in a decade or a century or even two centuries. There are still great new Civil War sources out there to find, to transcribe, to publish, and to use. We can and should increase our efforts to find and publicize these sources, so that we can better understand our greatest president and the greatest crisis in our nation's history.

Introduction

by Jonathan W. White

In 2006, I published an essay called "An Unlikely Database" in *Perspectives on History*, the newsmagazine of the American Historical Association, in which I argued that eBay is "an unprecedented research tool" that scholars should utilize. I described the shame I felt as a graduate student admitting to one of my professors about how I had found a historical source on eBay, but I nevertheless knew that eBay was such a valuable "database" that I wanted the historical profession to make good use of it. It was, I said, "an ever-changing 'library collection'" that "offers a dynamic catalog to scholars who are patiently and persistently willing to wade through it."

Now, 20 years later, we are fortunate that William J. "Griff" Griffing has been working with an eBay seller to "patiently and persistently" transcribe documents and make them available through his website, Spared & Shared. (In the essay that follows, Griff describes his process of transcribing the documents before they appear on eBay.) The selection of Griff's transcriptions in this book offers an invaluable and intimate portrait of Abraham Lincoln and his times, from the Lincoln-Douglas debates in 1858 to the presidential election of 1860, the secession crisis, the Civil

War, emancipation, Lincoln's reelection in 1864, and the fateful assassination at Ford's Theatre. The information contained in these documents would be lost to the public were it not for Griff's foresight and generosity.

Lincoln scholars, Civil War buffs, students, and general readers will find much of value in this book. Included are never-before-seen accounts of the president giving speeches, reviewing the troops, and even lighting up cigars with Union soldiers. Through a selection of more than 200 excerpts from letters and diaries written by the men and women who lived during the Civil War era, readers also get an in-depth view of the politics of the time. Many of the writers loved Lincoln, while others reviled him. In some cases, Union soldiers wavered in their support of their commander in chief depending on how the war was going at a given time. Some of the writers remarked that Lincoln was a good-looking man, while others called him ugly. Along the way, readers encounter many of Lincoln's Cabinet members, including William H. Seward, Salmon P. Chase, and Edwin M. Stanton; generals like Ulysses S. Grant, Henry Wager Halleck, and George B. McClellan; politicians like Senator Stephen A. Douglas, Vice President Andrew Johnson, and Speaker of the House Schuyler Colfax; newspaper editor Horace Greeley; and members of the Lincoln family, including the president's sons and First Lady Mary Lincoln.

The voices in this book bring Lincoln and his world back to life in ways that few sources do so many years after his death. Buried in private collections—and discovered as a result of Griff's 15 years of hard work—these long-lost voices are brought together here for the first time, giving readers a new perspective of our nation's greatest president.

About Spared & Shared

by William J. Griffing

Though I dedicated my career to energy research, I couldn't resist the allure of American history, especially the Civil War era. What truly resonated with me were the firsthand accounts from those who lived through the war and felt its profound impact. This fascination led me to eBay, where I discovered pieces of American history being bought and sold in the form of letters and diaries. It struck me as a travesty that such significant content was being circulated among collectors without being shared with the wider public. Fueled by this frustration, I searched for a way to extract the historical gems from these private collections without disrupting the trade. On a whim, I proposed to a high-volume eBay seller that I transcribe the letters and diaries before they were listed for sale. I offered to provide the transcriptions and my research for him to use in his eBay posts, asserting that it would highlight the importance of his listings and thereby boost the auction prices. I pledged to provide this service for free as long as he authorized me to preserve my work and the scanned images of the documents on a website. To my surprise, he agreed, and thus, Spared & Shared was born.

Some 15 years later, I'm still transcribing letters for this source, but no longer exclusively. Other sellers have sent me letters and diaries to transcribe in recent years, as well as a host of private collectors who have had no intention of selling on eBay or any other platform. Most of these correspondences were penned during the Civil War, though there are also a significant number of antebellum letters. This previously unpublished material has proven to be a goldmine for authors seeking fresh content and for family history researchers unearthing new relationships or dismantling long-standing "brick walls" in their genealogy charts. Beyond that, it has afforded me a gratifying hobby during my retirement and enabled me to meet others who share my passion for history.

Note on Method

Most of the initial transcriptions in this book were done by William J. Griffing. Griff selected excerpts from letters on Spared & Shared that dealt with Lincoln and sent them to Jonathan W. White. White then expanded some of the selections, and added a few other unpublished accounts that he had found in archives and libraries around the country (the sources for these accounts are cited in the notes).

During the summer of 2024, White worked with his highly talented student, Lainey Pratzner, to proofread Griff's transcriptions against the scans that are posted on Spared & Shared and the subscription database Research Arsenal. In editing the letters, they sought to strike a balance between readability and preserving the spelling and grammar of the original writers. Most of the letters were written by literate people and therefore required minimal intervention. In these excerpts, they silently added punctuation (or omitted superfluous commas), sentence breaks, and paragraph breaks. They retained common misspellings from the era (such as "fiting" for "fighting," "Sumpter" for "Sumter," "could of" for "could have," or various spellings of secession), as well as quaint misspellings that give a sense of the writer's voice (such as "keept," "evry," "vetrans," "tord" for "toward," or "litt" for "let"), but silently corrected careless misspellings and random capitalizations that might prove confusing or distracting to modern readers (such as changing "haveing" to "having," correcting "their" and "there," or replacing "to" with "too").

In some excerpts, when writers were only semiliterate, they transcribed the letters exactly as they appear, with many phonetic spellings and very little punctuation. (These excerpts usually begin with a lowercase word.) While these excerpts might take more patience to read, they give readers a sense of the writers' unfiltered voices. For the sake of readability, the editors inserted five blank spaces wherever a period should have been.

In all but the semiliterate letters, the words "Union," "North" and "South" (when referring to the regions), "Republican" and "Democrat" (when referring to the political parties), and the names of days have been capitalized, and ship names and newspaper titles have been italicized.

In both the literate and semiliterate letters, the following rules were followed as closely as possible: misspellings of Lincoln have been retained (such as "Linken" or "Lincon"), as have common misspellings of other prominent persons, including George B. McClellan, Ambrose Burnside, John C. Fremont, and Clement L. Vallandigham; compound words have been rendered as they appear in the original letters (such as "every body" or "to day"); duplicate words have been silently omitted; numbers and numerals are rendered as they appeared; abbreviations, including for state names, military ranks, and words like "regiment," have been rendered as they appeared in the originals; and possessive words and contractions that omitted the apostrophe are rendered as they were written (such as "dont," "Lincolns," or "enemys").

Readers who want to see the unabridged letters can find them at Spared & Shared or on Research Arsenal. Because of the editorial method employed here, the transcriptions in this book differ in some instances from the transcriptions that are available online.

Much of the annotation was drawn from the superb genealogical research provided by Griff on Spared & Shared. Brief biographical information for civilians is included in notes. Regimental information is included in the byline for each soldier. Notes have been created to identify major figures, as well as people who appear multiple times. Some less significant or infrequently mentioned figures are identified using brackets in the text.

The editors are grateful to the Office of Research and Creative Activity at Christopher Newport University for funding Lainey Pratzner's work on this project through a Summer Scholars grant. CNU's Center for American Studies also provided support, for which we are grateful. Finally, thanks to Todd Stephenson, Curt Witcher, and Jessie Cortesi of the Friends of the Lincoln Collection of Indiana and the Rolland Center for Lincoln Research at the Allen County Public Library for graciously providing images from the Lincoln Financial Foundation Collection.

Sen. Stephen A. Douglas, Lincoln's chief political rival in Illinois in the 1850s, was the northern Democratic candidate for president in 1860. (Library of Congress)

1858

"Politics were when I left home[1] and I suppose are still raging in Illinois. The canvass is by far warmer than '56. Three big men are ranting up and down the state—Douglas,[2] Lincoln, and Trumbull.[3] There are three candidates for Congress in our district (the fifth). They are now on the stump. Little Dug will have his hands full notwithstanding his opposition to the Lecompton 'swindle.'"[4]

– Michael Robert Buttz, student,
Northwest Christian University (now Butler University),
Indianapolis, Ind., September 19, 1858

Mathew Brady took this photograph of Lincoln in February 1860 when Lincoln traveled to New York City to deliver a speech at the Cooper Union. (National Portrait Gallery)

1860

"Hurrah for honest Abe of the West, Flat Boat, Rail Fence, and all. Now Frank, don't you think this paper is 'sum.'[5] There is everything being done that will tend to create excitement in this part of the country."

– J. Jones, citizen, Illinois, June 10, 1860

"Business is about so so but old *Abe* will make it right. The Travelling Candidate[6] made a short stop here but got awffully skunked in Maine. Free Tickets mustered 9000, the next day the rail splitters [Lincoln supporters] had over 30,000—the greatest meeting ever held in that State."

– John Byrns, citizen,
East Cambridge, Mass., August 20, 1860

"There is danger of L. [Lincoln] carrying this state—This I hold would be a great political calamity to the Union—for there are a majority of conservative votes here—but being divided at the polls—victory will perch upon abolition, so says your old friend."

– John Wilson,[7] attorney,
San Francisco, Calif., September 26, 1860

"Four years more have rolled around and they present to us Abraham Lincoln & Hamlin.[8] The abolition element has gained strength and has fairly shown its hand—a powerful party—a party which has no existence except at the North—is attempting to gain possession of the government with the avowed intention of administering it for the exclusive benefit of the North and in a spirit of hostility to the South."

– George Washington Wortham,[9] citizen,
Buchanan, N.C., October 10, 1860

This print of a Lincoln and Hamlin campaign banner, published in 1860, featured an American eagle, the White House, the Bible, and a copy of US laws. (Library of Congress)

"The Wide Awakes[10] are having great times here now over the Pennsylvania Election. They are going to Boston Tuesday evening to the torchlight procession which will be a grand thing. They have got another new Wide Awake company called the Lincoln Guard. Their uniform is a red cape and black cap. They look well, I tell you. I shall not go to Boston, but Father will and all the rest in the store. I shall stay at home and tend store. I tell you that '*Honest Abe*' is going to be the next President of these United States."

– Albert Freeman Dow,[11] citizen,
Lawrence, Mass., October 14, 1860

On October 3, 1860, thousands of Wide Awakes campaigned for Lincoln in a torchlight procession in New York City. (Collection of Jonathan W. White)

"Politics is quite lively here now. 'Old Abe' seems truly to be the 'peoples candidate.' Lovejoy[12] and several other celebrated men have spoken to very large crowds here, and tonight Sam'l Galloway[13] speaks in the 'wigwam.'"[14]

– Frank Gould,[15] citizen, Chicago, Ill., October 27, 1860

"The Northern mail has just reached us bringing election news from N. York, Penn., N. Jersey, Ind., Ill., &c. &c.—of multitudes for *Honest Old Abe* of the West. The citizens look grim & their faces are mightily elongated. The murmur is the 'Philistines have us.' I hear no appeal for discussion. I can't tell you how N.C. has gone, no news, 'don't reckon they done voting yet in the pitch pine woods.'

"Mason, I tell you I wish I could give vent to my feelings tonight in words with a good company of N.H. boys. But in bondage there is no freedom of speech.[16] There is no fear of Disunion though the Palmetto State may try to bolt, but their '*blasted*' cotton crop will not allow them to do much.

"The Old Buck & Breckinridge[17] Postmaster here I understand says he shall try & '*hold on*' notwithstanding Lincoln's election. I guess most of them will try & '*hold on*' & be right glad to hold on smart—don't you reckon? This town gave Bell[18] 213, Breck 152, Douglas 55. I did not vote at all for good reason that I need [not] tell you.[19] I hear tonight that [Anson] Burlingame has been defeated in Massachusetts by [William] Appleton, Whig. That fact must make the Rep's mourn a little, I guess."

– Joseph Brown Abbott,[20] citizen,
New Bern, N.C., November 7, 1860

"Rumors in papers today that S. Carolina will secede. That she has already taken steps so to do. That Governors of various Southern states have advised Secession, and reprisals on Northern states. My opinion [is] that it all results from temporary excitement and will soon tone down. At any rate our President must and shall be inaugurated, whatever it may cost. The government will be sustained by the whole force of the North, and by all in the South who remained true to the Union."

– William E. Potter,[21] citizen,
Princeton, N.J., diary entry for November 9, 1860

"But the result of the Presidential election has made it impossible. The effect of that disastrous event is to chain everybody here to the soil for the present as fast as Prometheus was chained to the rock. In the course of a few months, I hope to change my location for Huntsville [Alabama], or its vicinity.

"So far as I can see now, I can't discern any probable satisfactory solution of our present troubles without many throes & convulsions.

"Our news here is that S. Carolina has seceded, or resolved to do so, and that Georgia, Alabama & Mississippi will soon follow.[22] In such a state of affairs there will [be] great trouble in this and the other border slave states arising out of differences of opinion as to proper action. My own opinion is against State action or the partial action of a few states, but that a Convention of all the slave states should be held as soon as possible to determine authoritatively the mode & measure of redress. Let us all hang together, for we need all our joint influence & strength. So far, however, as the large majority of Virginians is concerned, I know they have no fear of Lincoln because they know his incompetency to administer the government, the heterogeneous composition of his party, the discordant & irreconcilable elements of which it is composed, and the general fickleness of the popular voice which in every Democracy changes with almost every election. We, therefore, would not in the Union apprehend any very serious consequences from this election, but still we will unite with the South in any effort made for our common interest and protection. Is it not therefore all-important that our counsels should be joint and our action the same?

"I fear that there are extremists at the South who will precipitate action and thus introduce the seeds of division at the South, whereas there should be unanimity from the Pennsylvania border to Mexico on that part of every State; and there will be, if a Southern Convention is held, and firm & at the same time judicious measures adopted.

"Before this reaches you, however, the die may be definitively cast, and States committed to instant & unqualified secession. In that event, though I can see nothing but ruin ahead, my destiny is with the South come what may.[23] With a melancholy but firm & undaunted spirit, I will take up arms against the sea of troubles trusting that Providence will vouchsafe to us a happy issue out of all our afflictions. Such will be the sentiment of Eastern Virginians, but I fear that west of the Blue Ridge we should have trouble, for there the slaves are few and far between. . . . The public sentiment here is extremely feverish & excited, and I would like to know your opinion of the action of Alabama."

– William T. Early,[24] mayor of
Charlottesville, Va., November 10, 1860

"Monday night Mary and I went down to the Monthly concert. The meeting was very small and as it was the evening before the election there was a great commotion outside. The Republicans fired their little cannon just by the church and such a deafening sound I never heard. The whole house shook. I thought I would go crazy it made me so nervous. Mr. Jennings did not continue the meeting on account of the confusion. Tuesday [was] the great election day. I staid at home all day in the evening. . . . Wednesday morning we heard of Mr. Lincolns election. We were disappointed, for we had hoped that such a man as he, without the least knowledge of state affairs, without any polish of manners, would not be sent to be the representative of this great nation, but so it is, by illegal voting &c. he is elected our President. I tremble for our country. I hope foreigners will not judge us all by our great head. I hope he will keep the peace, but I am afraid that our Union has commenced to break and will soon fall to pieces, but God knows what is best and we can leave all in his hands. The Republicans have all been victorious, they have carried our state, county, city and every thing else. Of course we are disappointed, but I have tried to cherish no ill feeling. I have been cheerful, and have not felt unhappy at all. I do not care much. I like disappointment some times. I know how to bear it, it does me good."

– Anna Ridgely,[25] citizen,
Springfield, Ill., diary entry for November 11, 1860

"News are a drag, nothing new at all,—times are 10 times harder than they have ever been, in fact this and last month have been the dullest we experienced since 1855. Lincoln's elected, Curtin's elected,[26] in fact, the whole Black Republican force have carried the Free States. The Republican Party will either 'make or break' this winter. If we get a *Tariff* through their influence, they are a party forever, if they don't there'll be no party under the 'cognomen' of Republican. And what is Lincoln, but a Minority President. He was not the choice of the People of the U.S.—he was only elected by the North. He has no power whatever. The House of Representatives & Senate being largely against him, he will not have a 'Bed of Roses' to sleep upon."

– Frederick W. Lauer,[27] citizen,
Pottsville, Pa., November 13, 1860

"and there is a grate excitement about the president that was elected some are almost scared to death While others onely laf at them but i for my part i ditent loose any sleep about it yet but i dont [know] but what we will have hart times if the south dont cool down before the forth of March [inauguration day] for the Way the papers say, they are going to kill the new elected president and if they Will do that then it Will give hard times but i guess they Will cool down yet before that time   but all this fus Would not have bene if that old John Brown[28] Would have kep his fingers out [of] the harpers fery scrape   but that mate the south sponky and now they are determint to dsolve the union   and i for my part cant plame them much for the black republican barty uset the south very mene to [so?] that i cant blame them very much   but stil it would be beter to cool down then to desolve the union."

– Peter J. Miller,[29] citizen,
Bridgeport, Ohio, December 23, 1860

1861

"I fear the consequences should there be war between North and South—what is to become of us all? For my part I can safely say if the Abolitionist[s] dont kill us, we will find a stopping place the other side of [the] Red River, but I hope for a satisfactory Compromise that will be permanent and then every abolitionist that crosses the line, kill him like you would a sheep killing dog. They are getting saucier every day. They all that talk here hear what we think of them. Will makes them mad occasional[ly] by telling them what they are doing and what he intends to do if they go to fighting. If possible, we will [illegible word] to Texas this fall though you need not say anything to any one for it is uncertain. Times are harder—if possible here since old *Abe's* election than ever—the Banks have failed [and] every man has lost money, that is, if he had any."

– Lizzie Fisher,[30] citizen, Bement, Ill., January 6, 1861

"I have little hopes of anything valuable being done while Old Buck[31] remains at the head of affairs, he is certainly a pitiable old cuss. Were it not for the high position he holds, he would be beneath contempt, but let us patiently await the fourth of March. Then, if the South will

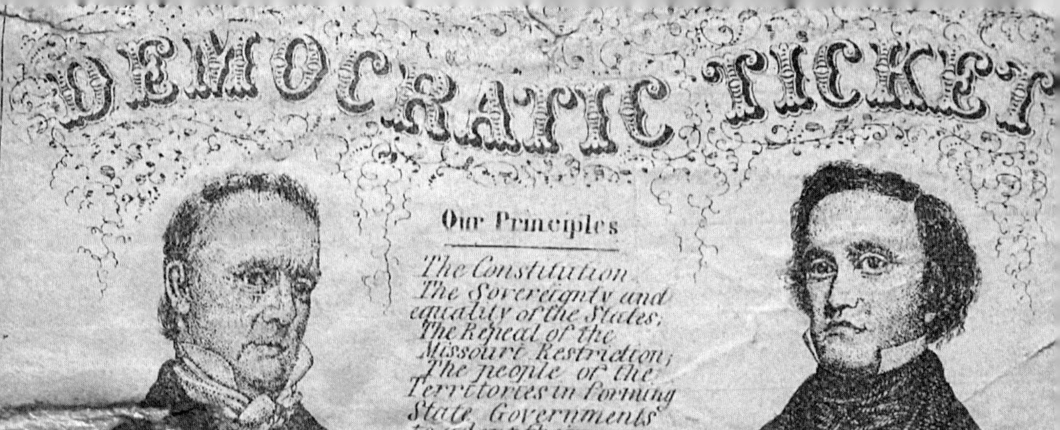

DEMOCRATIC TICKET

Our Principles

The Constitution
The Sovereignty and equality of the States;
The Repeal of the Missouri Restriction;
The people of the Territories in forming State Governments to adopt their own institutions

Lith of Ritchie & Dunnavant *Richmond, Va*

FOR PRESIDENT
JAMES BUCHANAN
of Pennsylvania

FOR VICE PRESIDENT
JOHN C. BRECKINRIDGE
of Kentucky

ELECTORS

1st	*District*	E. W. MASSENBURG	of Portsmouth.
2d	*do*	THOMAS H. CAMPBELL	of Nottoway.
3d	*do*	A. HUGHES DILLARD	of Henry.
4th	*do*	JAMES GARLAND	of Campbell.
5th	*do*	JOHN GOODE, Jr.	of Bedford.
6th	*do*	ALEX. JONES	of Chesterfield.
7th	*do*	WM. B. TALIAFERRO	of Gloucester.
8th	*do*	R. L. MONTAGUE	of Middlesex.
9th	*do*	JAMES BARBOUR	of Culpeper.
10th	*do*	J. RANDOLPH TUCKER	of Frederick.
11th	*do*	JOHN T. HARRIS	of Rockingham.
12th	*do*	A. G. PENDLETON	of Giles.
13th	*do*	JOHN B. FLOYD	of Washington.
14th	*do*	SAMUEL L. HAYS	of Gilmer.
15th	*do*	SHERRARD CLEMENS	of Ohio.

Write your Name on the back of the Ticket

be good enough to let Mr. Lincoln occupy the White House, I think we shall have better times."

– Judge William Brown,[32] Carey, Ohio, January 10, 1861

"I do not like the idea of a dissolution of the Union but if it cannot remain together unless we bow in submission to the slave power then I say let the bond be severed. This slavery question has just come to the crisis I have wished it to come to for years. It is not now whether slavery shall be protected in the territories but whether it shall be recognized everywhere and the right to hold property in man denied nowhere.[33] Nor is it the election of Lincoln or our refusal to protect slavery in the territories that alarms the South but that the public conscience of the North has been awakened and has taken form for once in political action.

"It is the public sentiment that chose Lincoln an exponent of itself. Lincoln's election is a finger-board pointing to the way the event has come. It is a weathercock showing which way the wind is blowing.

"'*Slavery is wrong*'—that is the sentiment in the North today and in a country like ours where public sentiment is almost law, it is no wonder the South trembles and grows white with rage. Death does not more relentlessly follow its victims to the grave than the roused spirit of Freedom will advance forward to the complete extinction of the crime and folly of human slavery.

"I believe Seward[34] uttered nothing more than the truth when he said there was an irrepressible conflict[35] between North and South on this question. Each have their vital principle. The North Liberty, the South Slavery. The question is which must give away. The principle of the one or the other must fall to the ground.

An 1856 Democratic ballot for James Buchanan and John C. Breckinridge. (New York Public Library)

Secretary of State William H. Seward. (Library of Congress)

Either Liberty must discrown her fair head or oppression shrink and veil its head and depart. We cannot compromise with them (the South) without giving up our own belief, our own principles, and our own honor."

– Robert McKee Gaston,[36] citizen,
Mount Pleasant, Pa., January 18, 1861

"We also intended going to Mr. Lincolns reception [on February 6], when he intended bidding his friends farewell . . . a remarkable day surely. . . . We found the house[37] crowded but did not know many of the persons as all of our friends had been there earlier and gone to a little dance. We did not stay long. I had some conversation with Mrs. Lincoln. She was dressed in a pear-colored moire antique with pearls and point lace. Mr. L really looked handsome to me. His whiskers are a great improvement, and he had such a pleasant smile I could not but admire him. At nine o'clock the street was lined with visitors, and many could not get in at all. I was glad we went later on that account."

– Anna Ridgely,[38] citizen,
Springfield, Ill., diary entry for February 10, 1861

"Lincoln reached here yesterday—I think he would do his country much better service, by going direct to Washington as soon as possible, than by travelling all over the country, making visits and foolish speeches."

– Henry P. Hubbell,[39] citizen,
New York City, February 20, 1861

"How do the Republicans in Indiana like the complexion of things by this time? Old Abe gave them a little hint of *Coercion* in his Indianapolis speech.[40] Since then his speeches, if they can be called such, convey to my mind, and I think to many others, his utter incapacity for the duties of the office to which he is elected. He arrived in N.Y. City yesterday, with comparatively very little excitement—less enthusiasm, and is now at this hour I presume, at the City Hall, not far from my office, shaking hands with those of the citizens who choose to call for that purpose. My curiosity to see the man does not lead me sufficiently strong to go to the City Hall, and he will probably leave tomorrow unseen by me unless by accident.

"As I intimated to you before, and as I firmly believe now, Abm Lincoln will be the President, and the government under him will be the government only of those states who cast their votes for him—the Northern free states. Every day's proceedings at Washington or elsewhere, and I watch them closely, convinces me that the whole 15 slave states will be a unit in a Southern Confederacy within two m[onth]s. And I don't think the people can be brought to adopt civil war for the purpose [of] coercing the seceding states. Our government is not strong enough for such a purpose—it never was framed upon the principle of military power, but upon the sentiment of the people. I don't well see how the Southern States could do any different than to claim proper guarantees for their rights before acknowledging a government brought into power against their consent and against their threats & entreaties on a platform & principles directly at war with their domestic institutions."

– Nathan Howard Jr.,[41] citizen,
New York City, February 20, 1861

New York City Hall.
(New York Public Library)

Left: **During his visit to Manhattan, Lincoln addressed a crowd from the portico of the Astor House.** ***Right:*** **Lincoln met with New York City Mayor Fernando Wood at City Hall on February 20, 1861. (Lincoln Financial Foundation Collection, courtesy of the Allen County Public Library and the Indiana State Museum and Historic Sites).**

"'Old Abe' has come at last. I tell you his '*brethering*' are making a deal of fuss about him and the '*Prince of Rails*' (his son Robt). I saw the 'old fellow' at a distance and was told by some that were close to him, that his portrait is far better looking than he. If that be the case, he is very handsome—over the left. You may form some idea of his looks by simply calling to mind Mr. *Isaac Vernon*, who is a finer looking man than '*Abe*.' He'll do now, won't he?

"I'll leave him now and tell you of something else. I went in Barnum's Museum yesterday and saw the 'Turkey'[42] that 'Abraham' is to have for dinner on the 4th proximo. It is a very large one and I expect is very *fat*. I hope he'll enjoy it as much as I would one of smaller size at Pa's table in company with you all. I must not dwell upon this point because I'll excite your desire to see me unintentionally.

"The Paymaster that is most likely to succeed us is one of 'Abe's' company. His clerk came down this morning to get some letters that had been forwarded 'to the care of Mrs. Leslie.' I do not care how soon we are relieved, I assure you. I wish it could be tomorrow or by the 1st of March at furthest. I must not be impatient."

– John Booton "Boot" Hill,[43] Paymaster's Office,
New York City, February 20, 1861

"Only limited number of tickets having been issued to admit persons to the [New Jersey state] Capitol, there was of course a great demand for them. Through the kind assistance of [state representative] F. F. Patterson Esq. I was admitted as a special Reporter, on the platform close to the chair of the President of Senate. Adjoining me were the Philada Committee, who had come thus far to meet Mr. Lincoln.

"Mr. Lincoln and part of his Suite entered about 12:15 and was introduced to [the] President of Senate who welcomed him in a short address. Mr. Lincoln in a finely modulated voice replied, speaking of his early interest in the revolutionary struggle in New Jersey, &c. in a speech of between five and ten minutes in length. He is a very tall man, standing if I am not mistaken about six feet three inches high. His countenance bears the impress of grave and earnest thought, as well as of great coolness and determination. But when he begins to speak, his whole face lights up with one of the most pleasant and heartfelt smiles that we have ever seen. I pray the Supreme Being who presides over the destinies of nations, and of individuals, that this grave, earnest, thoughtful, determined man, may prove, if need be, a second Washington to our Country. If there be anything in physiognomy, and experience has proven that there is, he is the man for the present crisis.

"Mr. L. dined at the Trenton House. Our party left Trenton at 1:32 P.M., arriving in city about 3 ½ P.M. Elmer, Riley, and I go to [the] Continental [Hotel]. Mr. Lincoln arrives in Phila about 4 P.M., and at Continental about 6 P.M. makes short address from balcony to vast crowd assembled in front of Hotel. Evening receives citizens in parlor of Continental. I retire early, i.e., about 12 P.M."

– William E. Potter, citizen,
Princeton, N.J., diary entry for February 21, 1861

"This morning at sunrise, Mr. Lincoln raised American Flag to staff over Independence Hall. I do not go, on account of crowd."

– William E. Potter, citizen,
Princeton, N.J., diary entry for February 22, 1861

"On Thursday Grandfather and I went down to the city in order to get a glimpse of the new President. In the afternoon we went to Rev. John Street's [at] Sixth above Brown and had a very good view of him and the cavalcade as they came down Sixth Street from the Depot. After supper we started out with the intention of going to his reception and stayed at the Guard House with Uncle George P. until nearly eight oclock when we found that the street was completely blocked up with people and that there was no possibility of getting to the Continental, so they let us out the back way and we returned to the Hotel. At the Guard I saw Ex-Gov. A. H. Reeder[44] of Kansas who is a singular looking short round man wearing spectacles.

"Yesterday morning before light we left the Revere [House at 227 North Third Street] thinking we would get to the State-house early and obtain a good position—however we found that quite a number of people had collected, and we placed ourselves on the State-house steps and expected to have a good view of all the proceedings as the platform was only a few feet in front of the steps. But when the crowd had become very large, they brought two or three divisions of police and began to clear us out. Gen. [William F.] Small told us we must leave the steps—Grandfather remonstrated with him but all to no purpose, and so we were compelled to leave and got jammed up with our backs against the wall about twenty feet from the platform.

"The police had a great time driving back the crowd in front—they threw themselves on them with their maces and were nearly ten minutes in effecting it. It was the largest multitude I ever saw, perfectly solid, and extending as far as I could see. For some time before seven oclock we could hear them clapping and shouting within the Hall, which sounded very pleasant, but that was all the benefit we had of it—however at that hour Mr. Lincoln made his appearance surrounded by a number of functionaries who almost obscured him. We saw him make a speech and afterward at our request (I mean the crowd's) the lesser celebrities quit the stand and almost left him alone in his glory. He took off his coat and hat, seized the rope, and the flag ran up to the top of the State House very easily and prettily without any hesitation or accident to make the omen a bad one.

"Rumor said that Lincoln was a horribly ugly man and rumor never told a greater falsehood—he is quite a good looking man with some resemblance to his photographs but very little. He has dark hair & whiskers. I believe every one who saw him was favorably impressed with him, and we made our way out of the crowd with high hopes and expectations and doubtless feeling very patriotic. Grandfather thinks he's a Henry Clay."

– Samuel W. Pennypacker,[45] citizen,
Phoenixville, Pa., February 23, 1861

While in Philadelphia, Lincoln raised a flag outside Independence Hall (shown here). In an impromptu speech, he stated that he would "rather be assassinated on this spot" than surrender the principles of the Declaration of Independence. (Library of Congress)

Admiral Hiram Paulding.
(Naval History and Heritage Command)

"I am just about to retire at eight & in the morning seek an interview with the President Elect. I send the enclosed by which you will see I am permitted to receive from Nicaragua if the President assents. What else has been done I will learn as soon as I can."

– Admiral Hiram Paulding,
Washington, D.C., February 24, 1861

"This evening I spent at the house of Judge [Stephen A.] Douglas, [naval officer Maxwell] Woodhull having taken me there in his carriage after dinner. I have had a private interview with Mr. Lincoln & a very pleasant call upon the lady who I think will fill her place acceptably."

– Admiral Hiram Paulding,
Washington, D.C., February 25, 1861

"Mr. Lincoln seems to be very favorably received at Washington. The personal qualities of the man are gaining him many friends."

– William E. Potter, citizen, Princeton, N.J.,
diary entry for February 28, 1861

"From the papers today, things look peaceable at Washington. I see that some of the most ultra Republicans are now coming out against Coercion. They begin to see such a course will never do. That was a rapid trip of Lincoln's to Was[hington]: from Harrisburg. I however look upon the Rumor of an attempted assassination as a Hoax.[46] So do most of us here."

– Charles Augustus Greiner,[47]
citizen, Savannah, Ga., March 1, 1861

This anti-Lincoln cartoon by Adalbert J. Volck depicts Lincoln's inglorious trip through Baltimore as president-elect in 1861. (Library of Congress)

"I meet with much civility by the Republicans of distinction & have no one to complain of but Mr. Seward—against him I fear I shall bear malice for a long time to come.

"It is like summer here & the dust in clouds. Tomorrow [the presidential inauguration] will be insufferable if there is not a change. I think I will not mix up with the crowd to go to the Capitol.

"There is great dissatisfaction amongst the Virg. & Md politicians in regard to the Cabinet as it has been named. My friend Mr. Seaton[48] told me in confidence that he had seen Mr. L. [and] told him he had the Union in the hollow of his hand. That if his Inaugural was not satisfactory to the South & his Cabinet were as now stated, Virginia would cecede in less than five days & the other Border states would go with her. Mr. Montgomery Blair[49] is indicated for the Navy. He told me yesterday if he went into the Dept. he wanted me here to assist him & be Sec. de facto. I replied to him that I could not afford to live here on my pay & that he would have to get an additional appropriation to support me—that with all my acknowledgments for the compliment I was better off on my farm. He said he would give me his at Silver Springs.[50] He is an able man & I found him civil. He told me that I had been his choice for Sec. of the Navy & many others say the same."

– Admiral Hiram Paulding,
Washington, D.C., March 3, 1861

"I shall go to Washington pretty soon to see what the new administration will do for us poor fellows, about 20 in the immediate neighborhood where I settled that is in the same fix with me about their titles. Of one thing I are very certain—we cannot have a worse government than we have had, for from the time of Adam down in any age or Country, a more corrupt and rotten government than old Buchanans there never was. This very day, thank kind Heaven, the old public functionary retires, and I hope President Lincoln will make a thorough cleaning out of the Augean Stables, and turn out to the last one, the most corrupt set of unmitigated Scoundrels there is in this or any other Country ever produced."

"I had hoped and expected that the Hon Schuyler Colfax[51] would have a seat in President Lincoln['s] Cabinet, but I may be disappointed."

– Levi Clark,[52] citizen,
Newark, N.J., March 4, 1861

Speaker of the House Schuyler Colfax of Indiana. (Library of Congress)

"President Lincoln's inaugural arrives today. It is eminently conciliatory, though firm in its tone, and seems to be received with favor by men of all parties. He takes the position that he will invade no state, but that he will collect the revenue, and hold, occupy, and possess the property of the United States. The address is characterized by great ability, as well as conciseness. Its general effect cannot be anything but pacific."

– William E. Potter, citizen,
Princeton, N.J., diary entry for March 5, 1861

"Our annual town meetings come off tomorrow all through the state. I think 'old Abe will win.' As far as Secession is concerned, I wish that all the slave states might be set off together so that we might have a *free* country if twas not so *large*. In regard to fiting the South 'and whipping them in to the Traces' as they tell about, I have not much courage for that. (Not but what they deserve it and I should like to shoot some of them well enough) but it would be fiting to *gain* just what I want to get *rid* of, so all I can do is to hope and pray that they will stick to Secession and that the border states will join them and that finally a convention of all the states will be called and vote them out of the Union, but I fear that war is inevitable and that we shall see bloody times. In case of a war, I should not be surprised if the South were victorious at first if not in the end, for they will be fiting for what they call liberty and for their homes, while our soldiers will be as the English were in the [American] revolution, fiting for *pay*. If war comes, we must let the regular paid army do the fiting but must arise one and all and strike for *real liberty* now and *forever to all mankind*, or there is no use in fiting at all."

– James Webster Carr,[53] citizen,
Manchester, N.H., March 11, 1861

"you seem to say that Old Abe is the man for us. I think that his election has caused more distress in the countrey than is possible for aney pen to relate, the hundreds and thousands he has been the means of starving to death and will be is all most a bomin bale [abominable] it would have been a good thing for the countrey if him and all the nigers were in hell if you were here to express your sentinents you would not stay more than a few hours and [if you] had to live a mongst niggers you would soon change your opinion. But since it is so it is all right if you can live under the present administration."

– Robert Elliott,[54] citizen, Granby, Mo., March 14, 1861

"we at last bid fairwell in Political friendship, never to meet until this nation & contry is drenched in blood unless you turne from the error of your way and quit following *such* [a] heartless demigauge *as Andrew Johnson*[55] whos speech is like himself, black as hell, nothing but slander and a disgrace to the state and age in which he lives and is endorsed by all the d—d black hearted Ab[olitionists] in the north. I do believe if hell was raked and sea scumed their could not be another such a D— heartless Hypocrit found, Judis not excepted, yes a Bennadict Arnold to give up his contry. Oh! may the gods be angry with him, may they blast all his efforts and aimes, may they cut him dow[n], O may Mars be upon him and send him down to his propper place and may his posterity if imbibed in his doctrines be blasted from off the face of all the earth, may all his seed be forgotten among men & those who will now say amen to his hellish notions, he has allways be[en] an Abolition[ist] in my opinion, and as he thinks that it is gitting popular he will now show his hand. Abe [Lincoln] is a gentleman to all such and would be prefferable to him with *me*. I hate a *traitor*.

"perhaps you begin to think I am a secessionist. Yes Sir that is my Stripe and as spotted with it as a leopard and say *dam* a man that hasent got the spunk to say Amen to it. . . . The only kind of Union you can be for is the union of the rases i.e. the Malgamation[56] of the *saxon* & the Ethiopian which is contrary to the laws of God and should be repudiated by all honest men. . . . The north firs[t] violated the law by passing the Liberty bills[57] which were unconstitutional and to repeal those law[s] would have been civil war & subjugation. And to have those laws remaining on their statute Books would be no Union at all, for a Union that is not in unison is no Union at all. Where can you see Union in their measures? The only chance to have Union is to go the way Wade[58] & Chase[59] & Greeley[60] go, Confiscate the property of the south. The Abolition[ists] are for Union, A Johnson is for Union. Therefore A Johns[on] and his Confederates are Abolitionists."

– Wyly J. Smith,[61] child, Lindley, Mo., March 24, 1861

"You ask me if I saw Mr. Lincoln while in New York? I did not, as I happened at that time to be more profitably engaged; besides I never like to look upon suffering humanity if unable to render assistance. You say that he is a 'great & good man.' Of this I know but little as his past record is much too meagre for me to base an opinion upon. He should combine both these qualities, as his position requires the possession of both, if good results are to follow. You ask what I think of his policy as thus far developed? This can be answered in a few words; he has not developed *any* policy yet; has refused to do so up to this moment, and consequently no opinion can be given. We are just now, like a man at sea in an open boat, tossed about at the mercy of the wind & wave without oars, rudder, or compass, and with no land in sight, or friendly hand to save him. . . .

"Our only hope for maintaining the unity of the states is for Mr. Lincoln & cabinet to adopt a policy of peace and concession, and give them all the property now located in their confederacy. Let not brother be arrayed against brother, but let peace forever exist. Obnoxious measures can never be crowded down the throats of Americans if dastiful [distasteful?], and I never wish to see one section commanding obedience over another by the power of the sword. Alas, alas, for our dear country. My heart sickens and feels sad when I reflect upon the pitiable condition [to] which bad men North & South have reduced her. It would seem that the people no longer have any master minds to lead them as in days gone by, & to embody in their public acts the true sentiments which pervade their hearts. The administration up to this hour has done nothing & seems uncertain what policy to pursue. I much fear it will eventuate in war upon the South—if so, God only knows what the result will be. May He avert it and save us forever from shedding each others blood. But enough of this painful subject."

– Dan Westervelt,[62] citizen, New York City, March 29, 1861

"I had a letter from John Paulding of Peekskill asking me to assist him in getting a mail agency & sending some very good recommendations from people whom I do not know. It is just in character with a foolish fellow unfit for the place. I must nevertheless try what I can do. The President is inaccessible to all but small politicians."

– Admiral Hiram Paulding, Washington, D.C., April 2, 1861

"I have understood that you want about 1000 men to come down to South Carolina and join the army now stationed there. If such is the case I would like to know as I have about 150 men under my command that have become disgusted with affairs here in

New Jersey, and would like to get out of this place as soon as possible. . . . I will give you an account of our proceedings here, and how our company began to form. In the first place, Abe Lincolns election was received by us with disgust. We immediately resolved to hold secret meetings here in Newark to see what we could do in regard to helping our Southern Brethren in case they should secede. The crisis has now come. If it is true that you need the services of our men, we shall come down to you at the first word that you send."

– Edward N. Fuller,[63] editor of the *Newark Evening Journal*, Newark, N.J., to Gov. Francis W. Pickens of South Carolina, April 2, 1861

"The order was sent from the War Department to the officer commanding the artillerists on board the *Brooklyn* to land with his men at Fort Pickens, but as no order was sent to the Capt. of the *Brooklyn* he would not land them. The President was much chagrined & will send a messenger overland & orders by water. I suppose the expedition that sailed yesterday from New York is destined for the relief of Fort Sumpter—I fear they have waited so long, that they are not strong enough.

"The gov't should risk nothing but always strike with an irresistible hand. I think we may now consider that peace is at an end. The people of the north west have compelled the President to go forward & are ready to march with a host whenever the first blow is struck. There will be a new era in the future which it is sad enough to contemplate. The Navy with the exception of the African Squadron[64] will be withdrawn except here & there a ship & all will be employed at home if necessary."

– Admiral Hiram Paulding, Washington, D.C., April 7, 1861

"I think South Carolina has been rather hasty and committed many wrongs and blunders and I fear will give trouble where ever she goes, though I hope I will be mistaken, but between her and the Republicans I am for her or anybody else. I hope if Sumpter is not given up soon, she will be taken and all who go to help her and if a fight begins, I hope Washington will be taken and all the Black Republican concern and keep them prisoners until peace is declared. I thought until yesterday that Jackson put down South Carolina in 1832, but such was not the case, for Mr. Clay brought forward a Compromise Bill that Calhoun accepted though reluctantly though it was a change from the original Tariff.[65]

"I hope every Southern State will Seceed if Lincon attempts coercion and whether they do or not, Thousands from all the Slave States will join the Southern Army to prevent Coercion and that every Repub[lican] who goes there to help coerce will never get back."

– H. W. Morgan,[66] citizen, Carlisle, Pa., April 9, 1861

"You will perceive that the Failure of Mr. Seward's shameful enterprise is as I predicted, only a little worse.[67] If such a thing is again undertaken whilst I am here in the same way, I shall ask to yield my place & this I intend to convey to the President as soon as I have an opportunity. We may know something more about it when we hear by water. As yet we learn by Telegraph in the hands of the South."

– Admiral Hiram Paulding, Washington, D.C., April 15, 1861

"I write you early in the morning as the only time when today I shall have the least chance. After my line of yesterday, I arrived here at 6 P.M. & having made report to the Sec. of the Navy,[68] went to the President who had Seward, Blair, Smith[69] & Chase with him. Thence I returned to the Department & by 9 P.M., we had Telegraphed & written, getting three hundred men & officers on the move tomorrow for Norfolk to get the vessels from the yard that are in a state of readiness to move."[70]

– Admiral Hiram Paulding, Washington, D.C., April 19, 1861

"We have just heard of the Bombardment and Surrender of Fort Sumpter; all is the wildest excitement. If the Arkansas Convention was in session it would Secede before night. The South will *all* oppose *Old* Abe's *Coersion* Policy, So *likely* you will hear that I am a citizen of another government before this reaches you. My heart sickens at the recital. I turn away in sorrow and anguish. Oh my unhappy and distracted Country—'tis for thee I mourn.'"

– Clement Hayden,[71] citizen, Maysville, Ark., April 21, 1861

"The events of life are rapid in these times. I was scarcely 24 hours in Washington before I found I was again to visit Norfolk on a mission of no doubtful character and after two or three interviews with the President & Cabinet & Genl Scott,[72] I embarked in the Steamer *Pawnee*. In 18 hours I was at Fortress Monroe & soon afterwards had a Regiment of [3rd] Massachusetts Volunteers which with the Marines I had brought made my command more than six hundred men."

– Admiral Hiram Paulding, Washington, D.C., April 22, 1861

"I went to Mrs. Stewart's the other day and had a *good* talk. I just feel like going right to *see* everyone I hear favors the South, for my heart goes right out to them. Someone gave Katie[73] a Union flag the other day, and I told her at first she should not have it, but she begged so hard and I could not explain to her then *why* I did not wish her to carry it, so I let her have it. As we were going home, she was running along before me and I stopped to speak to Nettie Stewart. I noticed some lady stop Katie and talk to her for some time and when I came up with her, I asked her what the lady said to her. She says, 'So little girl, you are for the Union, are you?' 'No mam,' says Katie, 'I am for Bell, my Mama said I should not carry this flag at first, but a little girl gave it to me and I begged her to let me keep it, but *I* am a *Southern[er]*.' '*I ain't* for Lincoln,' she always says whenever she hears his name mentioned."

– Katherine Pinckard, citizen, Indianapolis, April 23, 1861

"The war has been inaugurated & may continue to rage with a fury hitherto unknown. We have heard of the Alpha which was painted in flattering colours but who of us can describe the Omega. The first battle [Fort Sumter] has been fought and termined [terminated] in cheering results. It was miraculous & miraculous because bloodless, but shall this description depict the final struggle? We would all wish that such would be the case, but our wishes are of small moment. That a war policy would have been adopted by men of understanding appears superficially at least to be preposterous, but this Lincoln & his advising host have done [so]. I am of opinion that were their brains microscopically examined or chemically analyzed, they would be found deficient or at least made up of an unpure material so that were they weighed in the balance they would be 'found wanting.'"

– Unidentified "Dan" to uncle, Augusta, Ga., May 1, 1861

"Everything is down to the lowest point, no currency good for anything. If a man has anything to sell he dare not take money for it for fear it will be worthless next day, but we hope when 'Honest Old Abe' has won his laurels times will improve."

– Lydia (Judd) Stockwell,[74] citizen,
Tipton, Iowa, May 4, 1861

First Lady Mary Lincoln in 1861. (Library of Congress)

"I have just come from the barracks in the [City Hall] Park, where the volunteers were drawn up in line around a square space, & Mrs. Lincoln walked inside, reviewing them. She is quite fine looking, but was—shall I tell it? oh my!—*painted—much*, too!"

– Unidentified "Charlie,"
New York City, May 17, 1861

"Today I saw a Regiment of Germans & the Garibaldi Italians march in review before the President at his mansion. Can anything more be said than this—They are the victims of European Despotism, come here for liberty & in their exile here in free America alas! must fight for freedom. Alas! Alas! What a page for the Historians in the time to come. . . .

Secretary of the Navy Gideon Welles, whom Lincoln called "Neptune." (Library of Congress)

"I should enjoy your company, that of the children, home & the farm of all things else just now, and my mind would not be divested of its care for I feel too deeply the importance of restoring to ourselves, to our children & humanity the integrity of the government & subduing to obedience to law and order our unfortunate & misguided as well as our rascally countrymen.

"If everybody was like my chief [Gideon Welles] it would take some time to do it & perhaps a Tartar would be caught. The old humbug wears his beard about a foot long, white as snow & a monstrous wig that covers his whole head & I might almost say shoulders. Then he speaks quick & with a half impediment like & you would be amused to hear him raise his voice when I do not understand & ask him to repeat. Sometimes I make no reply on purpose although understanding perfectly well, to hear him in an elevated tone repeat what he had said before. I wish he was back in Hartford. He is not the man for the place—I am getting very tired of him."

– Admiral Hiram Paulding, Washington, D.C., May 30, 1861

"Washington is just now the most quiet place anywhere to be found. It is only when a Regiment arrives & is marching in review by the Presidents mansion, or when they are leaving for Virginia, or Rebel prisoners are brought to the Head Quarters of Genl Mansfield,[75] which is just opposite to the Department, that we have much of the stir of war. The ships of the Navy will all be officered tomorrow & nearly every officer on the Register assigned to duty & then in ten days they should be all at sea."

– Admiral Hiram Paulding, Washington, D.C., June 2, 1861

"You express surprise that Tennessee should change her position taken in February, yet what else can she do? We can but regret the present condition of our country, knowing and feeling that let things go as they may we are a ruined people, while we have had no hand in bringing about this awful state of affairs. On the contrary [we] have strove to avert it, believing that the preservation of the Union was the palladium of our liberties. But the North has by unfriendly legislation,[76] the press, the pulpit, and a good portion of her citizens goaded and insulted the South, driving them as a last resort to seek peace and safety in secession, a policy advocated by Mr. Lincom, an inherent right a people had he said, in a speech made in Congress in 1848, to secede.[77] He surely has grown wiser or weaker, now to deny a people a right he said was due to a people, but tis *then* and *now*, with Mr. Lincon or circumstances alter cases. . . .

"Tennessee does not endorse secession, but claims the inherent right to rebel against the policy of fighting her southern brethren and whipping them back into the Union where she would gladly remain, but never help to force an unwilling people to go with her That fated policy of coercion, subjugation, was indeed a fatal stroke, that which has driven the other border states out of the Union and tis that which will induce every true Tennessean to cast his vote for Independence on the coming morrow."

– Unidentified citizen,[78] Madisonville, Tenn., June 7, 1861

"We was visited day before yesterday by the president, honest old Abe as he is called, and I should think he might be honest, at least he is homely enough to be honest."

– Stephen Millet Bragdon,
5th Massachusetts Infantry, Alexandria, Va., June 16, 1861

"We cannot wage this war without money. Mr. Lincoln is calling for a large amount, but I think stands much less chance to get it than Mr. Davis.[79] As to his 400,000 men, he will have to double the number before he can hope to make an impression on the South. In less than 30 days we will have nearly that number (400,000) in the field. And there are 10's of thousands only waiting to see our country invaded, to fly to arms."

– Horace Moore Polk,[80] citizen, Bastrop, La., July 15, 1861

"We received glorious news here last Wednesday of the great battle at Manassas stateing that our side lost 5,000 and the yankeeys lost 15,000. Our side only had 15,000 and they had 35,000. I tell you it was a glorious victory. Jef Davis and old Scott was in the Battle, old Abe was not their and you never wil hear of him being wher the Dixie Boys can get a shot at him. I think if I *ever* get to see the young man, I will try my old musket at him and if he was not very smart I think I would get his scalp."

– Charles L. Dupree, 7th Alabama Infantry,
Warrington, Fla., July 27, 1861

"Went to Chain Bridge Aug 20th. Visited the camp of the 33rd [New York], Col. [Robert F.] Taylor. In the afternoon witnessed a review by Genl McLellan[81] of Gen [William F] Smith's Brigade.[82] The 31 Reg'ts composing the Brigade were formed into line—open order—and McLellan and staff rode through scrutinizing closely every man. He is a fine looking man but has been so much exposed to the hot August sun that he is browned like a Texan. President Lincoln, Sec't

Seward, Cameron,[83] [and] Chase were also present and witnessed the firing of the battery which commands the river and the Bridge. Lincoln is as rough and unassuming as when he was an ordinary lawyer in Springfield, Ill.

"'Pigmies perched on Alps
"Are pigmies still!'

"Sect Seward I have always had a great curiosity to see which was fully gratified. He is a different looking man than I had imagined him to be—with a full-leaf-Panama Hat which concealed the whole of his countenance but his interminable & exhaustless nose. He resembled a moderate sized Toad sitting under an overspreading cabbage leaf.

"Sec't Chase is a fine looking man and has a look of intelligence. Of Sec't Cameron I could not look at him without thinking of Pennsylvania R.R. Speculations[84] & what excellent roads they were to transport the soldiers to Washington—superior to all other[s] in the Union. And then again what great facilities his friends in Philadelphia had for manufacturing clothes &c. &c. No other city could begin with it. And besides, what an excellent place to select Generals from—Excellent. *Glorious institutions of ours—and giants to administer the gov't.*"

– Henry S. Joy, 3rd New York Cavalry,
Washington, D.C., August 20, 1861

"we are expecting to haft [have to fight] every day but we dont know when it will be but they will halve some trouble to wride over us all for there is a good meny of us when we are all to gether we was out on drill the other day and there was about tenn or fifteen thousand Soldiers in the field and old abe linken was there and he went all a round the field and we all had a good chance to see him and after he was around we all gave him three cheers and it mad[e] a good deal of nois i a sure you."

– George Bender, 1st Pennsylvania Light Artillery,
Washington, D.C., August 25, 1861

"the Bregade to whitch our Regi[ment] belongs was drawn in lind of battle and inspected by the president and Wm. Sewert and three Magor Generals and the 24 reg got the praise. I was not able to go with the boys so I did not have the honour of seeing those gentlemen. I have not told Mr. Lincoln what you wished I should."

– Theodore Holmes, 24th New York Infantry,
Arlington Heights, Va., August 28, 1861

"Mr. Lincoln reviewed us last Monday & after the review he came to our camp & examined our rifle cannons. He thanked us very kindly for our gallant conduct at the battle of Bulls run & when he went away he went up to where our cook was getting dinner & took a brand of fire & lit his cigar & sit down and had a long talk with our captain. He is a very pleasant talking man any one would not think he was president of the United States if they did not know who he was."

– John Fales, 3rd US Artillery,
Arlington Heights, Va., September 5, 1861

"Fremont *alone* has met the question and handled it as God would have it handled and [the] government will probably remove him for it.[85] Seward is a mighty *humbug* and Lincoln is his willing tool. Neither of them meet the crisis like *men* nor Christians, but like politicians who dare not say their souls are their own."

– Daniel Burdick Maxson, 4th Wisconsin Infantry,
Relay House near Baltimore, Md., September 23, 1861

"I expect to be at home to take dinner with you on New Years Day as I think the war will be over by that time. Old Abe went past here last Friday evening. Just before he came along, there was a company of artillery came along and fired a salute of ten guns and when Lincoln came along the boys broke past the guards and surrounded him and gave him three rousing cheers and then called for a speech but he said this was no time for speeches. He said he would make them a speech when the war was over. This was the first time I had seen him."

– David Walker Beatty, 63rd Pennsylvania Infantry,
Washington, D.C., October 6, 1861

"We had fine times last Sunday [October 6] when the President and Mr. Seward reviewed us. I think that Abe is a good looking old fella for the cares of his office are wearing upon him. He seems very shy and reserved. God bless him and the old Bay State."

– Richard Whittock Clink, 11th Massachusetts Infantry,
near Bladensburg, Md., October 7, 1861

"I saw Presadent Lincon riding out   I thought he was qite a good looking man."

– Orville Robinson, 9th Maine Infantry,
in Maryland near Washington, D.C., October 16, 1861

"I have just been reading the address of Mr. Breckinridge to the people of Kentucky[86] & am perfectly inflated with a mixture of enthusiasm, anger, and indignation. It is the finest document of the age—and I believe will find its way to the minds & hearts of the sensible, brave & patriotic portion of the people of that state. I have the utmost confidence in the final redemption of Kentucky from under the tyranny & oppression of Lincoln and his miserable myrmidones[87]—and when I think of the outrageous treatment of ex-Gov. Morehead[88] & his compatriots whose hands are manacled & whose hearts are bleeding under the wounds of Tyranny & oppression—I feel a desire inexpressible to aid the true gallant sons of Kentucky in defending their homes & liberties and in avenging the wrongs of their unoffending brethren."

– Capt. Meredith Kendrick, 3rd Georgia Infantry Battalion,
30 miles from Savannah, Ga., October 21, 1861

"as for my part I dont care much whare I go nor whare I am for I expect to be a soldier the Balance of my days for I cannot see anny happyness anny whare else Some times I think I had just as soon be ded as alive for hour country is ruined anyhow and what is thare on the earth that would make me want to live except my relations Cousin to think one man [Lincoln] and his crew can ruin this onst happy Country."

– William T. Davis, 4th Tennessee Infantry,
Columbus, Ky., October 31, 1861

"We had 120,000 men reviewed here last Wednesday[89] by Gen. McClellan, & Prince de Joinville,[90] President Lincoln, Seward, Cameron, and all the *Big Boys*. Beautiful sight it was. Only think, Old Abe was all smiles for everyone he saw. There was 100 pieces of nice field pieces on the ground & they would begin and fire them one after another in succession. I reckon there was a plenty of noise."

– Thomas Davis Peck, 5th Vermont Infantry,
Camp Griffin, Va., November 22, 1861

Prince de Joinville and friends with the Union army near Yorktown, Va., May 1, 1862. (Library of Congress)

The Lincoln home at Eighth and Jackson Streets in Springfield, Ill., in 1861. (Library of Congress)

"I have been around the city several times. It contains some 10,000 inhabitants. President Lincoln's residence is here, it is nothing more than common, 3 or 4000 dollars would build such a house."

– Cyrus Marble Cummings, 2nd Illinois Light Artillery,
Springfield, Ill., December 20, 1861

1862

"The majority of the naturalized Americans in Canada will do as much in this war, if it comes to that, as the natural born Canadians or old countrymen will. The impression is very general here that the present administration are convinced they cannot regain the Southern States and that to unite the Northern people and to in some degree make up for the loss of the South, they wish to go to war with England and if possible annex Canada to the United States. If such is their idea—and the fortification of the Northern frontier and the tone of the Republican press has convinced us of it, we Americans in Canada can feel no great sympathy for the government, for we cannot see that Canada would be anything but injured by a change. . . .

"The rebellion has been very differently managed by the two contending parties. One has committed the conduct of its Military affairs to thoroughly educated Military men. The other keeps the Military men, with the exception of McClellan, in subordinate positions and its Generals are chosen from prominent Republican politicians who, as may be supposed, know as much about Military matters as a cat does of his grandfather. This mismanagement has now prolonged the rebellion eight or nine months when it might as well have been stopped at first—or if the Administration knew, which they certainly did, what was the strength of the South, it would have been far better to have let the cotton states go in peace without a blow being struck, which if it had been done, would have saved several other slave states which have now gone besides the remaining ones which will yet go. It would have saved the country the financial ruin which is inevitably coming upon it, and besides would have avoided the lasting disgrace which will forever hang over the North on account of such performances as that at Bull Run.

"My own private notion is that the republican form of government in the United States is dead—and that we will never see another President. When a republican government rewards with a prison those who are politically opposed to it, and silences such newspapers as criticize its course or are opposed to it in principle, we may be sure that it is near its end. It is too much like the Old French Republic to last. There is likely a Napoleon in the army who when the proper time comes will clear out the Houses of Congress with his bayonets and take his place as Dictator in the White House, and when he has been that long enough will call himself King or Emperor. But even this to my notion would be better than President Lincoln's Government, for these people would be prepared for a Military despotism and would have the satisfaction of knowing that they had a clever man at least at the head of affairs and not such a ninny as Lincoln—nor such a babbling, blundering[91] ass as Seward. Mob rule whether you call it universal suffrage or what else you like is not a healthy rule nor one which promises to be lasting."

– Henry Augustus Sims,[92] citizen,
Ottawa, Canada, January 2, 1862

"I was down to hear Horace Greely Lecture last Fryday eve.—wee got there some time before the hour for the Lecture, but wee waited patiently until the house was full, then amid Cheers that made the great Building tremble, Greely enterd accompanyed by '*Old Abe*' and several members of Congress, also other distinguished men, the old man spoke well it was good, it seemed to meet the approbation of all present as they Cheered him at evry turn."

– Henry Clay Long, 11th Maine Infantry, Washington, D.C., January 5, 1862

New-York Tribune **editor Horace Greeley. (Library of Congress)**

"Was ever the fidelity and patient endurance of a devoted people more heavily taxed? All faith and enthusiasm is gone from the army—and hope only a glimmers afar off. With the news of the bombardment of Sumpter the enthusiasm of the country burst forth with irresistible power and within an incredible short period over one million of men were offered the president by the loyal states—Six hundred and sixty thousand were received and are now in the field. For what? To maintain the integrity of the Union and the supremacy of the Constitution? Or to be the dupes of a treacherous, imbecile, and cowardly Administration? 'Whom the Gods would destroy they first make mad.' If the destruction should be limited to those in power it will be well. Neither the army nor the people are at fault—but I fear the hand of futurity will point the finger of scorn at 'Old Abe' and say, 'Thou art the man.'"

Aaron Brown, 3rd Iowa Infantry, St. Louis, Mo., January 7, 1862

"I may enlist for 2 years or the war. I hope I wont have that to do, but it look very much like all of us will have it to do or litt Mr. Lincoln pollute the sacred soil . . . & you know we cant stand that."

– Thomas Radford Hollowell, 12th Tennessee Infantry,
Columbus, Ky., January 27, 1862

"We feel afraid here that Lincon and his wife have too many relatives in the rebel army.[93] Why did he modify Freemonts proclamation and then turn him out when he was doing more than all the rest? Soon after that, the story was McClellan was to be superseded but he was too cunning. He fell into the do-nothing policy and keept his post. Why was the white house gardener[94] promoted to a Lieutenancy? Look at the Potter Investigating Committee[95] and you will see why he should not [have] been. There are a great many things around Washington which looks dark. Why do they not clean out the traitors? If I had the control I would make every one of them pull hemp as fast as I could find them and it appears they are not hard to find, but the government is afraid of hurting them. I do not think it would hurt them long to make them pull a very little hemp. It appears there is a vast number of them there and the women—they that are traitors—are a great sight worse than the men."

– Ira Cole,[96] citizen, Fowler, N.Y., February 6, 1862

"There are no families of small children in this place that I know of except of the class called '*poor whites*,' and they are poor indeed, for they seem not to realize the cause of their poverty. Our revolutionary fathers were poor, and the oppressions of the Mother Country were calculated to make them poorer, but they had intelligence—enough to appreciate the cause of their distressed condition. But the masses here are made the victims of misrepresentations from the political leaders who compel the people to dig their own political and social graves. Thousands of men are now fighting in the ranks of the rebel army who are the ignorant victims of a lie. They are made to believe that Lincoln is conspiring for their destruction. Their leaders tell them that the Yankees desire only to destroy and pillage. But when they find it otherwise, they must feel an awful indignation against their leaders, & unless the unfortunate originators of this terrible rebellion are either killed or taken prisoners, an awful reaction must sooner or later take place."

– Surgeon Frederick Kinsman Bailey, 20th Illinois Infantry, Savannah, Tenn., April 18, 1862

"last saturday one of the boys in the Ken[tucky] 8th was on picket and [a] secesh came along and he halted him three times and he did not stop   then he went on accross his post and turned around and told him that he would not halt for no damnd lincolnite nor black republican son of a bitch and as the bitch came out of his mouth he got a bullet through his heart   it went in at his left breast and through his heart and rite lung and he droped [in]sensible."

– Horace S. Chapin, 9th Michigan Infantry, Murfreesboro, Tenn., April 22, 1862

"I had quite an affectionate parting with the President this morning. He told, as is his wont, a number of stories more or less decorous, but all he said having any bearing on political matters was: 'I suppose my position makes people in England think a great deal more of me than I deserve, pray tell 'em that I mean 'em no harm.' He does not pay much attention to foreign affairs, and I suppose did not like to talk about them without Mr. Seward."

– Lord Richard Lyons,[97] British minister in Washington, D.C., June 13, 1862

"I have Just heared of the Destruction of McClelans army Before Richmond, & old Abe has Called for 300 Thousand more Troops   the Lord onely knows when and where this damnable

Niger war will end or what it will Bring us to it seems that the Niger worpshers [worshippers] are Determined to ruin the Country in Taxes and loss of life."

– Dolphus Clark,[98] citizen, Manlius, Ill., July 3, 1862

"We have had considerable news from Richmond since you wrote, but it dont seem to amount to much except destruction of life and limb. I have some doubts about their ever accomplishing much so long as Lincoln is so fraid of hurting the Rebels or desturbing their Slaves or other property. I think he has much more Simpathy for the Rebels than Jef Davis has for us."

– George Quint,[99] citizen, Dover, N.H., July 17, 1862

"This morning the President has ordered that all the clerks in the different Departments form themselves into Companies & that they be armed to do duty in defence of the Capitol—under this order I fall into line at 11 o'clock—one hour from now—but you must not be alarmed as we suppose we will not be required, only to perform Guard duty in the city so as to relieve soldiers who are now on that duty. I shall do my duty the best I can. I do not know how arduous it will be—my health is good."

– Charles M. Heaton,[100] citizen,
Washington, D.C., September 3, 1862

"We saw by Mondays paper that the clerks were going as nurses to the battle field and that our army was whipped . . . and we did not rest much on Monday night. I was afraid you had gone to the battle field and I knew you could not stand the fatigue and the horrible sights you would have to see there. And we knew there were other dangers attending the battle field. But when we got your letter of last Sunday we all felt much better. I hope you will not have to drill too much for the Washington guard. I am sure you could not stand it.

"I go in for arming the blacks. I dont believe the South can be conquered in any other way and I can't see why negro blood should be held more sacred than the white mans. If I had fifty sons I would oppose evry one going to war under this rule of the administration. It would be much better to have the negro killed off than the white man. The president wants to get clear of the negro by sending him off to some other country.[101] I think he had better put him in the battle and save white men. It's awful to think of the condition of our country."

– Ann Crane Heaton,[102] citizen,
South Bend, Ind., September 6, 1862

"I think that these draw backs are in the fault of our Generals and not the President. I do not think that we could get another man more fit for the place that Old Abe holds than he himself. But I do think we could place [a] Gen at the head of our army more fit for that office than those that now hold that situation. Perhaps we have not. If so I think it is nearly time to give up the ghost."

– Theodore F. Ostrander, 58th Pennsylvania Infantry,
Portsmouth, Va., September 18, 1862

"The present Government was of your own choice and you ought to trust its ability and honesty of purpose. If President Lincoln says Emancipation let the People be a unit in supporting him. I think President Lincoln desires to execute the will of the People. I think he has striven to act so as to keep them a unit. In his delay in issuing the late proclamation,[103] I think he has accepted[104] its policy and the approval of the majority of the People. It is all twaddle about our inability to crush the Rebellion without interfering with slavery. Let us have united will and action and we must either crush it or acknowledge ourselves cowards and imbeciles. It *is* the fault of this faction who have left no means untried to thrust this one idea of Slave Emancipation upon the president—thereby embarrassing the government which has so long prolonged the struggle. They would displace the greatest chief of our armies today solely on account of party."

– Chaplain Joseph Edward Kimball, 8th Massachusetts Infantry, Fort Monroe, Hampton, Va., September 30, 1862

"There is a good deal of talk here about President Lincolns Proclamation to free all Negroes which is said to have passed but nobody knows anything about it. I cant find a man that has seen it but still they say it is so."

– George Henry Shaw, 3rd New Hampshire Infantry, Port Royal, S.C., September 30, 1862

"Drilled this forenoon in company drill. In the afternoon we were brought out in review (Col. [John R.] Brooke commanding) and formed in 'close column' on the heights. Just as we got into line a pelting rainstorm came on but soon after the sun smiled gladly upon us. A salute of 24 guns warned us that some high dignitaries were on hand. In a few minutes 'Old Abe' came riding down the line accompanied by 'Mac' and [his] staff. Round after round was heartily given to them as they passed from the enthusiastic soldiers. Long live 'Old Abe' and 'Little Mac.' They are the soldiers' hopes, and the pets of the Nation."

– James Wilson Barnett, 53rd Pennsylvania Infantry, near Harpers Ferry, Va., September 30, 1862

"Pheby we had a hard fight in MD[105] I presume you have red all abat [it] we had the plasure of having aC al [a call] from old abe and little Mcclain yastday old abe loked like a Shark more then like a man Mc is the one that loks the Best to us the boys like to sea him he loks good to them."

– Daniel Wiley Lafferty, 64th New York Infantry, Harpers Ferry, Va, October 3, 1862

General George B. McClellan in 1862. (Library of Congress)

"Weather exceedingly foggy in the morning but after the fog disappeared it was exceedingly warm for this season. We arose early. Were assembled for the reading of orders against pillaging. Were again assembled at 7 A.M. and marched to a suitable place to be reviewed by President Lincoln. General McClellan, Burnsides,[106] and many other generals accompanied him. We did not return until about 11 a.m. The President looks care worn. Working at my gun. Dress Parade. Some orders were read. Prayer Meeting."

– Christopher Columbus Lobingier, 100th Pennsylvania Infantry, near Antietam Creek, Md., diary entry for October 3, 1862

"Last Friday our corps was reviewed by the President accompanied by Gen. Burnsides, Gen. McClellan and staff, and a score of *spouters* from the White House. Old Abe looks very much like other men except he is the sleepy giant looking man that his pictures represent him. He seemed greatly pleased with the looks of the troops. Burnsides is the dirtiest, reckless, most careless looking man I ever saw, he had a shocking black old Kossuth hat pulled over his head and ears, he had huge side whiskers and mustache

Alexander Gardner captured this photograph of Lincoln visiting McClellan at the Army of the Potomac's headquarters near Antietam on October 3, 1862. (Library of Congress)

and an excellent set of pearly white teeth, his face, or the part of it not covered with hair and hat, was terribly tanned, he had an old blue nightgown on for a coat, and his pants were tucked into a pair of boots that were covered with patches, but he rode a splendid horse. Bully for him, he puts on no airs but looks worse than any private in the ranks. We'll back him up wherever he goes.

"McClellan is a young looking man with a full round face with no whiskers, but a handsome mustache and imperial, his hair neatly combed and he sported a fatigue cap with a light blue velvet band around it, his uniform was neat but not extravagant, his horse is the handsomest animal I ever put eyes on. The yells and cheers that the boys gave 'little Mac' as he passed were perfectly deafening."

– Charles Henry Howe, 36th Massachusetts Infantry,
Antietam Iron Works, Md., October 5, 1862

"The army was reviewed day before yesterday by *Old Abe* accompanied by General McClelland and his staff. The men looked well as they was drawn up for review, not withstanding the hardships they have passed through lately. As the President rode in front of our regiment (only

Survivors of the 44th New York at their muster-out on October 11, 1864, at Albany, N.Y. (Library of Congress)

numbering one hundred men), Gen. McClelland asked the President if he remembered the fine large regiment the 44th Ellsworths[107] that passed through Washington about a year ago. On being answered in the affirmative, he said this is what remains of them."

– Anthony G. Graves, 44th New York Infantry,
near Sharpsburg, Md., October 5, 1862

"president lincoln Was here the other day and if you ever see his picture you can see him for he looks just like it."

– Martin Van Buren Culver, 16th Connecticut Infantry,
Pleasant Valley, Md., October 12, 1862

"the whole camp is cheering the patriotick address of genneral mcllelan[108]   george B. mcllelan has more honnor in this camp than Lincoln and all of his friends   the whole blame lies in the men that are wanting office in the old regiments and they think they will do it at the cost of old Pennsylvania."

– James Drolsbaugh, 171st Pennsylvania Infantry,
camp near Harrisburg, Pa., November 7, 1862

"You would perhaps like to know what is thought of 'Lincoln's Emancipation Proclamation' by the soldiers in this army. It is endorsed by the majority of them, for they cannot otherwise be consistent with views expressed & held on other matters connected with the management of the war. The most of all those that I got acquainted with that were proslavery now say, 'God speed to it.' Yes, anything that will tend to end this unholy war. The Army is undoubtedly with the President, & when it gets home, it will settle with those that are at home misrepresenting them, & have not given this Proclamation a hearty support. I have just heard that Ill. has some against it. If our state had done as Iowa has done,[109] giving the soldiers a chance to express themselves upon the mighty & all absorbing subjects now agitating the public mind, she would have swept the whole state of Vallandigham[110] Traitors & politicians. But the results in those states that have accorded this privilege to them, will be proof to the world that the Army is with the Administration in its efforts to put down this rebellion."

– William Davidson McCord, 37th Illinois Infantry,
Marionville, Mo., November 8, 1862

"Well McClellan is gone from us, I am sorry to say. I think he is the best man in the country to lead an army but for the 3d time 'Old Abe's' courage has failed and again he yields to the d—d politicians of the fanatical school. What they expect to gain is more than I can see. They complain of inactivity and just as the army commences to move, they take away a leader in whom all have the utmost confidence. Why? The Abolitionists *never* meant that 'Mac' should take Richmond."

– Isaac Arnold Jr., 2nd US Light Artillery,
Manassas Junction, Va., November 16, 1862

McClellan taking final leave of the Army of the Potomac on November 10, 1862. (Lincoln Financial Foundation Collection, courtesy of the Allen County Public Library and the Indiana State Museum and Historic Sites)

"Father, you have the same opinion of *Old Abe* that I *once* had. I have *now no right to speak ill of the President or any of his subordinate officers* (See Regulations).[111] But this much I will say, that notwithstanding the hardships a soldier endures when the army is advancing, if the soldiers were allowed to vote, the Democrats would carry the day *ten to one*, and it was the earnest wish of the *old army* that all the States would go Democratic. Things now appear as if Abe was running his party ashore. I think that a change in the cabinet could be made for the better."

– Charles Henry Howe, 36th Massachusetts Infantry,
camp near Fredericksburg, Va., November 30, 1862

1863

"Last night about twenty of us saw the 'Old Year out & the New One in.' We had a jolly time. As twelve o'clock came around, we went in, 'en masse,' to where our 'Nig' 'Washington' was sleeping and awoke him, tossed [him] up & down on some shelter tents, pulled his wool, rolled him & after frightening him almost out of his wits, pronounced him in the name of Abe Lincoln & the Constitution, a Free Man.[112] Then such a shout & roar of laughter as we sent up over the once slave-then free man. It was rumored that '*he* didn't see the point.'"

– William Carlton Ireland, 44th Massachusetts Infantry,
New Bern, N.C., January 1, 1863

"the boys are all getting out of hart they haint verry willing to fight anymore and i will tell why lincolns last proclamation that he has distr[ib]uted out amongst his men tells that he is agoing to fight to have those black nigroes free and the biggest part of the boys swares that they will throw [down their] arms and go home if that is the case for what use is it for us to risk hour lives just on account of having those black free two Regt of the souths stacked armes and went home then they sent one Regt of cavalry after them to bring them

Secretary of War Edwin M. Stanton. (Lincoln Financial Foundation Collection, courtesy of the Allen County Public Library and the Indiana State Museum and Historic Sites)

back and they stayed at home also   and we heard that two of hour illinois Regments went home too and the govoner of pennsylvania says he will draw his men all in till spring and wont let a man fight any more if they wont settle before long[113]   but hour old ballheaded govoner from ohio[114] he is a going to give two hundred thousand more men."

– Jacob M. Buroway, 107th Ohio Infantry,
near Stafford's Station, Va., January 4, 1863

"I have had quite an opportunity of forming the acquaintance of big Generals and big officers of state. I visited the White House, shook hands with the President, looked at Mrs. Lincoln, surveyed the whole affair and was glad that I did not live in the establishment for greatness has its corroding cares. The President is an honest, patriotic man, but none too great for the occasion. Secretary Stanton[115] is a burly, English-looking, fast living man, rather puffed up by his position. Admiral (Commodore) [Andrew Hull] Foote is a plain, easy, sensible, practical, energetic man; I enjoyed his society much. Halleck[116] I have not yet seen, but he loves to have his hand on the helm."

– Chaplain Frederic Denison, 1st Rhode Island Cavalry,
Washington, D.C., January 19, 1863

"You say you wish you could believe the words of the old song which reads 'Might is with the right and the right shall be.' I do not know whether I wish to believe it or not for it is not a settled thing in my mind which is right. Jeff Davis prays that God will favor them, and Abe Lincoln prays that he will favor us, and I dont see but that Jeff's prayers are as effective as Abe's. I suppose you will think I am a regular 'Secesh' but you ought to hear the boys in our Co talk once. You would think all their sympathies were with Old Jefferson D."

– George S. Youngs, 126th New York Infantry,
camp near Union Mills, Va., January 22, 1863

"We want one man—& that man wants to be a good careful Gen & statesman & one that when he makes up his mind that a thing is right, to push it through & not be talked out of it by those who know nothing about the matter. Old Abe is nothing more than a tool. Seward is the best man that he has about him."

– Charles E. Bradley, 32nd New York Infantry,
White Oak Church, Va., February 1, 1863

"The boys are all much pleased with the Valentines received yesterday. Old Abe's, Chases, and such pictures make very acceptable Valentines with the soldiers."

– Asa Mulford, 11th Independent Battery, Ohio Light Artillery,
Memphis, Tenn., February 15, 1863

"I attended the Presidential levee yesterday & was introduced by [Lincoln's private secretary William O.] Stoddard to Mrs. Lincoln who said to her I was the gent who sent the fruit to them from Syracuse. She replied she remembered it well and that it was very fine indeed. And [I] just now met her upon the steps as she was going to her carriage for church & we of course bowed the usual recognition."

– Samuel Newell Holmes,[117] citizen,
Washington, D.C., March 1, 1863

"Every single rebel General of any note except [Nathan Bedford] Forrest and [John Hunt] Morgan were educated at West Point, but they have had an opportunity to carry on their campaigns on their own plans while every campaign we have had except one or two in the west have been managed solely by the politicians. Of one thing I feel sure, if the ultra politicians continue to rule over Lincoln and the War Department sixty days to 3 months longer the South will certainly achieve her independence. The North has not gained one point of value for eight months & today occupies actually much less of the rebel soil than we did six months ago, and the rebels

Secretary of the Treasury Salmon P. Chase.
(Library of Congress)

have probably added more men to their army than we have. If this conscription law[118] is rigidly enforced and the politicians will let Lincoln and the War Dept alone, I believe we shall succeed in the course of the year. I guess you will think I have croaked long enough, but although unpalatable what I have said are truths."

– Lt. Col. Calvin Waldo Marsh, staff of Maj. Gen. John M. Schofield, Springfield, Mo., March 4, 1863

"old abe wants to make another emancipation bill and he wont be no whare for the army are down on him for the one he passed it donte take here and the quicker he recalls it the better I think for fighting for niggers is aboutt played outt here they dont think enough of them to fighte and lose their life nor they wont much longer I have seen all I want of them and I dont think I shal fight much to free them they had better make it a war for the union and then the men will be better satisfyed."

– John R. Pollock, 149th Pennsylvania Infantry, Lincoln General Hospital, Washington, D.C., March 8, 1863

"There was a '*Union Supper*' over at Hocke's Hotel last evening. The way they come to have it there was this. One evening last week a number of these butternuts about town ([Judge Thomas Peter] Finefrock, [Bruce] Lindsay, and others) went over there to hold one of their meetings. They abused Lincoln and the soldiers and talked '*secesh*' so strong that Hocke ordered them out of his house. They remonstrated, but he told them to go. They then told him that they would get their horses and go and that it would ruin him. He told the hostler to get their horses ready as soon as he could and let them go. Said there was something in his heart that told him he ought not to let them do so and he would not have it. The Union men were so pleased when they heard it that about one hundred of them went over there last night and got their supper."

– Sarah Eliza (Wilson) Rice,[119] citizen, Fremont, Ohio, March 28, 1863

"I understand your regiment is agoin to reinlest again but dont you for god sake if you do it will kil me if you only knew how I count the days for your return you never wold punish me so and how glad I am when night comes to think that you [have] one day les to stay O if I can live to see you again you had better beleve that thay never get my consent for you to go to war again the devel coms thay cant draft you becaus old Abe has exempted A poor widow onley son."

– Sarah Ann Adams,[120] citizen,
Hollis, N.H., March 29, 1863

"With regard to the duration of the war, I think it will continue till the expiration of Lincoln's term of Office. It has been occasioned by fanaticism,—is prosecuted by fanatics,—and they will continue it, while they have the power, for they are blind, foolish, and mad."

– Willis Faulke Riddick,[121] citizen,
Richmond, Va., April 1, 1863

"I have no words with which to express my detestation of the course that John Furgeson is taking on the war question. What does he mean. I have no objection to his being a Democrat, but in the name of heaven, cant he be a Democrat, and still be a loyal man and a patriot? Why does he not side with such noble and true men as Gov. Tod, Dickinson,[122] Butler,[123] and Van Buren,[124] rather than be found ranged alongside of such as Vallandigham, Jeff Davis, Sam Medary,[125] Ben Wood,[126] and Co. You say that in his New Richmond [Ohio] speech, John asserted that Lincoln had violated the Constitution. Did he prefer any charge of that kind against the President of the Southern Confederacy? Or does he think him innocent of any violation of that instrument. He talks very hard about abolitionists. Does he say any hard things about rebels? He thinks that Democrats will be intimidated by military force, and perhaps be prevented from voting, at the next election. Does he think Massachusetts troops, who, he says will be the instruments in such work in Ohio; does he think they will interfere with *loyal* men while exercising the right of suffrage? It would seem that such would hardly be the case, especially in consideration of the fact—as they claim it—that a large majority of the soldiers are Democrats."

– Daniel Hayford, 25th Indiana Infantry,
Memphis, Tenn., April 7, 1863

"This Corps with three others was out on Review. I believe there was about 80,000 in all. President Lincoln reviewed us, he is the homeliest man I ever saw."

– Charles E. Carruthers, 17th Maine Infantry,
camp near Potomac Creek, Falmouth, Va., April 9, 1863

Lincoln reviewing the Army of the Potomac on April 6, 1863, by artist Edwin Forbes. (Library of Congress)

"went up west of here near Falmouth on Review (this being Wensday last) and wer Reviewed by Gen Hooker[127] & Old Abe I was on Camp Guard and did not go I saw Gen [Abner] Doubleday & his wife pass that day the Next day (being Thissday [Thursday]) I saw the sight it Was Lincoln and his Wife they were in A Covered Wagon drawn by four Horses & his son he was not as Large as Percy & was riding A Horse he was A real nice Looking Fellow they wer followed by Genral Hooker Sedgewick[128] and other Genrals and officers to Numerous to mention that we did not know they went down tord

Belplain [Belle Plain, Va.] to Review some Troops there when they came back we gave three Cheers for them first for Old Abe then for Hooker & then for Sedgwick & then we had to give three Cheers for Little Mc. I dont know what Hooker thought of us for giveing three cheers for McClellan but he is the first & the Last man that the Army of the Potomac will waist their breath cheering for but we would Cheer three times three if we could get him for our Commander Again."

– Altus H. Jewel, 77th New York Infantry,
near White Oak Church, Va., April 10, 1863

"We have been reviewed 4 times within the last 3 days and have had a chance to see all the big men that I ever heard of. First we were reviewed by Gen. Lee,[129] our Brigade Commander, next by Gen. [Nathaniel] McLean, our Division Commander, 3rdly by Gen. [Oliver Otis] Howard, our Corps Commander, and 4th and lastly by Uncle Abe, Gen. Halleck, Secretary Seward & Stanton, Uncle Abe's wife and 2 boys,[130] & Gen. Hooker with lots of other officers too numerous to mention. I tell you it was a big sight. I guess there was about 20 or 25 thousand in all, pretty good turnout for a general training. Wish you could of seen us. I tell you twas a splendid sight. Uncle Abe looked very care worn. Dont wonder that he should having so much on his mind, it is enough to make any man look care worn and weary."

– Sylvester Rounds, 17th Connecticut Infantry,
Brooks Station, Va., April 11, 1863

"general Thomas[131] has just come from Washington and maid a speach to us & he said that the negrowes is fre[e]d. he is sent to make up 20 thousand and he says that he will get them with out any trouble he has already raised 3 or 4 [Colored] rigments when he was done he ordered three cheers for linkern but the 26 [Missouri Infantry] dident cheer for him."

– David C. Jones, 26th Missouri Infantry,
Milliken's Bend, La., April 18, 1863

Lincoln's son Tad reviewed the troops with his father on several occasions. In this image, the rambunctious boy, sporting a Zouave uniform, drew facial hair on himself. (Lincoln Financial Foundation Collection, courtesy of the Allen County Public Library and the Indiana State Museum and Historic Sites)

"Abraham's war missile—the proclamation—has barred foreign recognition, tripped out the underpinning of treason's Bastile, and cut the hard knot of the problem of the age. One can hardly measure the scope and results of that duty-inspired—almost divinely inspired—measure. This is less man's war than God's war. It is a day for heroisms of every kind, political, military, social, moral—yes, every power and every quality of every member of the nation must be tried."

– Chaplain Frederick Denison, 3rd Rhode Island
Heavy Artillery, Port Royal, S.C., April 25, 1863

"I have just witnessed one of the lovelies seans of my life, thus. The funeral of a Negro Soldier and herd the prayer of a Negro for the first time. And in all the prayers I never herd a better prayer in my life. He went through all classes, Culler, and the President Lyncoln, his officers, and Army. Never shall I forget this Sabbath eve, the Negro on his knees pleading for his wife in bondage. I will tell you more about it some time next June with the blessing of a kind Providence."

– Benjamin Austin Merrill, 50th Massachusetts Infantry,
Baton Rouge, La., April 26, 1863

"Tuesday night May 5th the whole army recrost the [Rappahannock] river not becaus we wer whipped there but because Sedgwick Commanding the 6 army corps, he crossed down below Fredricksburg & took the hights & then left one Brigade there to hold them & started up the river where we wer fighting The rebes turned his flanks & obliged him to retreat acrost the river so you see the rebes had posesion of the hights. they say that orders came from Abe not to fight & endanger the capitol if that is so I would not care a bit if the capito[l] was burnt to the ground."

– Wilber H. Merrill, 44th New York Infantry,
camp near Falmouth, Va., May 6, 1863

“old Abe Staunton & Hallack is out here thay came here yesterday a great many of ours troops is demoralized I think that we need a new leeder in place of Hallack iff he cant moove the army to better advantage Hooker is not to blame for this thare is a nough of troops to whip the redel army iff thay was mange[d] right the way thay have been Doing is send in a squ[a]d and get it slaughterd then fall back this is neerly plade out with the soldiers we want a fore ward moovement of all the army then we will gain victories in place of Dafeets at all points.”

– Samuel Dunnan, 1st Pennsylvania Light Artillery,
near White Oak Church, Va., May 8, 1863

“Old Abe ought to raise about 600,000 conscripts and arm and equip them. Then we would get the rebs all into Richmond, surround them, and starvation would bring them to terms mighty quick. That’s the way to do it.”

– Enoch C. Dow, 19th Maine Infantry,
near Falmouth, Va., May 30, 1863

“I hope the war is done in Virginia. I want to carry it right into the heart of the enemys Country and let them feel the effects of invasions a while. We will show them, with Gods help, that we have more Jacksons than one.[132] *Lee* has the best army in the world. We can whip any army Lincoln can put before us.”

– Capt. Henry H. Roach, 21st Virginia Infantry,
near Sharpsburg, Md., June 19, 1863

“I have just heard to day of the removal of Joe Hooker from the command of the Army what in H—l is that for can you tell can any body tell only that he has not been able with an inferior force to defeat a superior, I am almost tempted to *dam* Abe Lincoln up hill & down for it I suppose that he has some reason for it or he would not have done it but it is discourageing, I had confidence in Hooker if he had been let alone   the war will never end in our favor if it is carried on as it hass been for the last year."

– Anson K. Mills, 23rd Ohio Infantry,
Fairfax, Va., June 23, 1863

"last sunday there was a man by the name of thomas Brown   he was cutting wheat and he had his boys helping him and some others and when they got done they all got drunk and got to fighting and quarreling and one of browns boys run another fellow off by the name of alexander hatten for hollowing hurrah for lincoln   and hatten started home and said he would kill three or four of the browns that knight and he got his pistol and butcher knife and went over to John browns and went to the window and John was in bed a sleep and his wife was not asleep yet   they was laying with their heads to the window and he snapped his pistol at browns head three or four times and it did not go off   and browns wife heard him and waked brown up and he cralled out of bed and got his gun and went out and snapped it at hatten and it was not loaded   and he run at hatten and struck him across the back and knocked him down and jumped on him and commence beating him   and hatten got his knife out and stabbed brown in six places   he cut him two the hollow across the bowels and his guts come out and he cut him to the hollow on the shoulder   whenever he breathed the wind would come out of his shoulder   he cut three of his ribs loose from his back bone   them was the worst places   brown is still alive and they have sent hatten to jail until court."

– Thomas P. Kirk, 82nd Indiana Infantry,
Brown County, Ind., July 18, 1863

"I council you in the name of God and a common humanity, in the name of your own manhood, and the posterity you love, . . . not to be led blindfold[ed] by a party who ignores the only constituted athority to save our government and lead it up out of this baptism of blood to a new consecration to the freedom of all men. If you have not the courage or disposition to stand by our government, for Gods sake dont assist the Rebels by your influence. You curse Lincoln and the American government over which he presides, but I have never seen even one Little *Dam*!!! for Jeff and his Rebbel Government—conscription—confiscation—high taxation &c.[133] Can it be? I can read nothing else in your communication. I hope you will review this subject candidly unimbiased by your political predjudices. Our Country weal or woe now vibrates on the turning of the scale of this grate rebellion."

– Warren Clark,[134] citizen, Gasport, N.Y., July 25, 1863

"The ignorant masses are easily led and excited as was the case with the N. York rioters,[135] but where was Vallandingham, Wood, Thain,[136] Jim Wall,[137] and others, out of harms way, after counseling them to resist the draft, and exciting their worst fears and passions by telling them Old Abe intended to make them fight for the niggers and make slaves of their wives and children. A friend writing to me from the North says he hopes I will soon be home to help hang the Copperheads (if not with hemp) with scorn and contempt."

– William Suydam, 9th New Jersey Infantry,
Beaufort, N.C., September 4, 1863

"Now about this war, there is no use of saying any thing about it. Old Abe took the job of putting down the rebellion and I engaged to help him three years and to risk my life when called on during the three years. I thought the cause worthy of that risk and still believe it to be a glorious cause, and that every free man should do all in his power to put down this rebellion and with it that great and wicked institution *Slavery*, but after all, if the old man does not get through with the job within about a year, I think that if I live, I shall return to civil life and let some one else take my place."

– Israel Markham, 7th Illinois Cavalry,
Lafayette, Tenn., September 9, 1863

Congressman Clement L. Vallandigham of Ohio was the most notorious antiwar Democrat. Branded a "Copperhead" by Republicans, he was arrested at his home on May 5, 1863, for disloyal speech and, after conviction before a military tribunal, was banished to the Confederacy. He spent the next year in exile in Canada before returning to the United States shortly before the presidential election of 1864. (Library of Congress)

"you wanted to [k]now what i thot a bot the war now i can tel you very qick it is a hard plas here but i dont think it wil last mush longer an for putin linkin in for 4 years mor tha cant do that not by a vot if he has a lexion he wont a gathen [gathering] vots in the arme an ask for the nigro voters that is not so a tol [at all]."

– William C. Johnson, 114th Illinois Infantry,
near Vicksburg, Miss., November 2, 1863

"The President's Annual Message has been lain before Congress, and it is sound to the core. We ought to be thankful that we have such an honest, upright, and able man in the Presidential chair. . . . I see that Mr. [Henry S.] Foote of Tennessee, a member of the Rebel Congress, has offered some resolutions before that body in regard to the exchange of prisoners which looks towards a recognition of our colored soldiers as such. I like the President's determination not to exchange unless every man who wears the blue uniform is recognized as a soldier of the United States."[138]

– William Oren Ensign, 14th Ohio Independent Battery,
Lynnville, Tenn., December 18, 1863

"I hope Brig. Hays may be successful in getting you home to Auburn, but I don't think he will do it. It is said Abe Lincoln has had the '*Small Pox*.'[139] You ought to ask for a pass to Washington to go and condole with him. He thinks it cant disfigure him."

– Thomas Stacey, 111th New York Infantry,
Clifton Springs, N.Y., December 22, 1863

1864

"We all went to Mr. Colfax[140] levee, Friday night. Oh how sorry we were that you & Mary could not be there—the house upstairs and down was crowded. Mr. Chase & daughters[141] & other dignitaries were there, and we had a grand time. Cary told me her Mother and herself the evening before had dined with the President & Mrs. Lincoln—she said from what she had heard of Mrs. Lincoln for some time past that she was prejudiced against her—but she says her prejudices have all been removed, that Mrs. L is a very pleasant Lady, and has the knack of making her company feel perfectly easy and at home. Cary also, on the invitation of Mrs. L, attended the Theater with her and was perfectly delighted."

– Charles M. Heaton, citizen,
Washington, D.C., January 31, 1864

"The expectation is universal that the coming campaign will be decisive: the North can not continue war on a scale so gigantic without hope of success. We can & must fight on forever, if need be; we fight for home & liberty; death would be preferable to defeat. They have no such interests at stake—they propose to conquer & to subjugate, and in the effort itself have lost much of their liberty and submitted to usurpations & violations of their constitution that I did never before believe a free

This cartoon depicts Lincoln in patriotic clothing while feeding a spoonful of "conscription" medicine to a stereotypical Irishman. An advertisement on the wall for "Dr. Lincoln's Ready Relief Pills" features a pile of cannonballs. (Lincoln Financial Foundation Collection, courtesy of the Allen County Public Library and the Indiana State Museum and Historic Sites)

A BITTER "DRAUGHT."

Entered according to act of Congress, in the year 1863, by J. HALL & Co., in the Clerk's Office of the District Court of the United States for the Southern District of New York.

people would submit to. The longer the struggle continues, the nearer they will approach to a despotism. Gold has risen to 1.58 & the bounties offered for soldiers range as high as one thousand dollars. The time to elect the successor of Abraham is not far distant. Mr. Seward must give some proof that the rebellion is likely to be crushed in the next three months, or the next three hundred years. The people of the North will not always be satisfied with promises. The Federal debt is already enormous—worse than folly to increase it—unless something is to be gained by the war."

– Capt. George Douglas Wise, aide to Maj. Gen. Carter L. Stevenson, C.S.A., Dalton, Ga., February 15, 1864

"if the republican party nominate Lincoln and they let the army vote[142] he would not get but a few votes in this regt for the most of them think he is trying to prolong the war they think the president can do any and evry thing it is of no use to try to reason with them I should think that one half the regt is dutch and irish and the rest or a good many are canallors[143] but most of the drafted men are more like human beeings one can talk with them with reason some of them are well read."

– Samuel Huntington, 100th New York Infantry, Morris Island, S.C., March 3, 1864

"Tuesday evening I went to the Presidents Levee, the first I have attended this winter. The evening was pleasant and the walking good. James Sample & myself went together, but notwithstanding we went early, we found the East Room & halls pretty well filled. It had been announced during the day that Genl. Grant was to be there. This called out an immense crowd—there were a good many Ladies there, yet the Gents outnumbered them five to one.

"I met Mrs. Green there, the lady who keeps the boarding house on 9th St., not the one that boarded at Mr. Finneys. She introduced me to a Mrs. Wait from New York State. I offered her my arm and we, with many others promenaded once around the East Room, and just as we got to one of those large sofas right opposite the Green Room entrance, a loud clapping of hands commenced and it was soon discovered that Genl. Grant was about entering the East Room. We saw that he was just entering along with Secy Seward. The crowd pressed toward him very heavy but he pressed his way through and crossed the room directly where we were. They came right up to where we stood. We shook hands with him, but the crowd pressed stronger & stronger to shake him by the hand. I spoke to him & Mr. Seward & told them to mount upon the sofa or they would be overwhelmed. Mr. Seward thanked me for the suggestion, and up they mounted, with their boots on the elegant sofa.

"The rush in that direction was terrible, and was impossible to get away from it, and I told Mrs. Wait to get on the sofa. She done so, and I put my hand against the wall, but the pressure on me was so great I could not stand under it, and I also mounted the sofa. By this time, Secy Stanton got there, and he also mounted the sofa. There was no controlling the crowd. They rushed from every direction & those that had shaken hands with the Genl. could not get away. I took it on myself to speak to the crowd and urged them to open the way on one side so that those who had shaken hands could pass off. Some was pressed to the floor, & they placed their feet against the sofa & pushed the crowd back—and in this way run their feet through the silk covering of the sofa, & about ruined it, tore it full of holes, large enough to run my head through—but we finally succeeded in opening a way for them to pass off.

"Mr. Seward spoke several times, and so did Mr. Stanton of how fortunate it was that they accidentally came to that sofa—or the crowd would have overwhelmed them—their position was fine for the crowd to see them. I was taken by hundreds for Secy Welles and it was generally remarked that Genl. Grant was accompanied with three of the Cabinet. Now dont you think I felt very much flattered over that? Genl. Grant stood there near one hour, with both hands extended, shaking hands with everyone he could reach. At first the Ladies could not get near, but after a half hour or more they began to come forward—and at the end of near an hour, the most of the crowd had succeeded in taking the Genl. by the hand and the press slacked off when Secy Seward & Genl. Grant left the room arm in arm. I then had a promenade with Mrs. Sturgis and a sister of Mr. Sturgis who is now there on a visit—and then I retired and went home somewhat fatigued with my evenings excursion. Mr. Haynes did not go to the Levee—and instead I believe he went to the office or to church, I forget which."

– Charles M. Heaton, citizen,
Washington, D.C., March 11, 1864

After Lincoln became convinced that Grant would not challenge him for the presidency, Lincoln promoted him to the rank of lieutenant general in a ceremony at the White House in March 1864. (Lincoln Financial Foundation Collection, courtesy of the Allen County Public Library and the Indiana State Museum and Historic Sites)

"You remember Mr. Colfax had determined not to be a candidate again, but the pressure has been so strong on him to withdraw that determination that he has about made up his mind to yield to the wishes of his constituents, & I have no doubt will again be a candidate. Congress will adjourn about the 1st of June, and he will be home soon after the meeting of the National Convention at Baltimore which takes place on the 7th June.[144] Mr. Lincoln will get the nomination without a doubt & will be reelected. Nothing can prevent it—the people and the soldiers are for him every where. Mr. Chase[145] has declined being a candidate in a very patriotic letter which has done him great credit."

– Charles M. Heaton, citizen,
Washington, D.C., March 20, 1864

"Business is very good, though we are not driven. I have just returned from a State Convention at Madison called to nominate delegates to the Baltimore Convention. Lincoln seems to have the inside track, though there is no very great enthusiasm for him. I would prefer Banks,[146] or Chase, & perhaps, Fremont. I think there is some doubt whether Mr. Lincoln will be nominated at Baltimore. I think I perceive a growing reaction in the minds of the people against him."

– DeWitt Davis,[147] citizen,
Milwaukee, Wisc., March 31, 1864

"Tomorrow evening is the last reception at the Presidential Mansion. We are all going and expect to have a gay time. I hope better success will attend our visit this time.

"We had just a good joke played on us last Tuesday evening. It was noticed in the paper the day before that it would be the last reception, so we concluded to go rain or shine. The gentleman had a carriage sent around and we went. All the time the rain poured in perfect torrents, but we thought, *what of a little rain*, but we were in a closed carriage and felt none of it. As we got opposite the [White] House [we] beheld nothing, not even a sentinel was to be seen, so we concluded *not* to *get out* of our comfortable quarters *just* to see *Mrs.* Lincoln—it was raining too badly. If we had looked at the paper that day, we would [have] seen that it was postponed on account of the inclemency of the weather. I saw it announced in the paper next day the President and family [were] at the theatre that evening.[148] They attend the theatre quite frequently. I went a while ago [and] saw The Seven Sisters played."

– Josephine Elizabeth Bunnell,[149] citizen,
Washington, D.C., April 11, 1864

Between 1861 and 1865, Lincoln hosted many receptions at the White House. (Lincoln Financial Foundation Collection, courtesy of the Allen County Public Library and the Indiana State Museum and Historic Sites)

"You seem to speak in yours that the Administration care more for the coming political campaign than to finish up this rebellion. We too like Pres Lincoln, the country will accord to him an honest heart, but I have wished some times that he had a little more of the Genl Butler about him."

– Calvin Gilbert Tilden,[150] citizen,
Middlebury, Vt., April 11, 1864

"I am Sorry to hear that so meney of my cousens are of the copper head Stripe and I hope they may see the errer of their wase and reform befour it is to late for it will be rathr a bad Name for the famley to bare after the matter is settled. . . . I think that General Grant[151] will settle thee difilunty [difficulty?] now soon and that my cousens had better repent soon while the dores are open and vote for old Abe so as to wipe out all stane on the famley, for now is thee time to repent, for the dores will be closed after [a] while and then thare will be no chance for them as they will of lived out thare day of grace and repentance will be of no avale to them then."

– J. P. Hughes,[152] citizen, Honolulu, Hawaii, April 17, 1864

"About president some of the Boys want Old Abe put in again and a great many do not There are a great many Vetrans that are in favor of Little Mc all that were under him."

– James Almon Jacobs, 1st Maine Cavalry,
Washington, D.C., May 8, 1864

"Isn't thee thankful that the noble fighting Army of the Potomac has at last a leader worthy of them—one who will preserve himself & them from the horrible Washington-torpor—by the smell of gunpowder & the roar of cannon—perhaps we may be thankful that '*the Honest*' wants to serve a second term—he dare not imperil that prospect by hampering Grant, though I dont doubt his Queen, if not himself, is quaking with fear lest Grant should make himself too popular. I suppose it is very dreadful for me to feel so when

President Lincoln 'is so honest & tells such pertinent anecdotes—and ________[153] is so honest,' but I cannot feel that honesty, rare as it is, is the only thing that is requisite in a leader, especially a leader who is to conduct us over such quicksands, through such bogs as lie in our future path—but God is over all, and it cannot be that He will suffer a *hollow* peace to arise over all these wasted lives, these broken hearts—no not *wasted* lives if henceforth our country is truly free."

– Anne (Robinson) Minturn,[154] citizen,
Waterloo, N.Y., May 15, 1864

"Mr. Lincoln will be nominated tomorrow. Genl. Grant is moving on to Lee's works—but the Telegraph will keep you posted."

– Charles M. Heaton, citizen,
Washington, D.C., June 6, 1864

"I see the Baltimore Convention have nominated Lincoln & Johnson for President & Vice President. I would rather some one else had been chosen. I do not think either of them possess the qualifications that the Chief Magistrates of our Country should be possessed with—but still there is no use of expressing any opinion, as I do not see there is any help for it. I want to see a gentleman at the head

At their national convention in Baltimore in June 1864, the Republicans nominated Lincoln for president and War Democrat Andrew Johnson of Tennessee for vice president. (Library of Congress)

of our affairs—but it seems such qualifications are a draw back. I am sorry they did not take up Grant—but we must make the best of it."

– Lt. James Cornell Biddle, staff of Gen. George G. Meade, Cold Harbor, Va., June 11, 1864

"I have been down to the Capitol this forenoon to hear Dr. Breckinridge from K.Y., an uncle of John C. preach.[155] His text was the 15 verse of the first Chap of the first Epistle of Paul to Timothy. The discourse was very interesting. There was the largest audience present I ever saw filling the Hall of Representatives. Abraham Lincoln was present with the members of Cabinet & many other distinguished men. The singing was congregational of old and familiar music which sounded Heavenly. Oh I wish you could of been there. The President came in shortly after services had commenced as sly as a cat. I dont believe there were forty persons in the House [that] saw or recognized him unless they were acquainted with him and their eyes directly upon him when he entered the door. He was dressed very common—not as cleanly as the general average of common folks. I saw him at the White House yesterday. He had just got out of his carriage all covered with dust & sweat. To day he had on the same suit. After services he arose from his seat and assumed his characteristic Indian gait and left the crowd as soon as possible, shaking hands with a few ladies acquaintances as he came in contact with them."

– J. Milton Whipple, 17th Independent Battery, New York Light Artillery, Washington, D.C., June 12, 1864

"From this place, taking a street car, we went to the Presidents house; were admitted into the Reception room—and now dont ask me to give a large view of it because I cannot. There were three large chandeliers hanging from the ceiling; two large looking-glasses on opposite ends of the room filling nearly the whole end, nice carpet, nice window blinds—in fact everything was in style. I seated myself and rested awhile probably on a chair that old Abe has sat on. I did not get to see Abe as he could only be seen at certain hours."

– David Davis, 170th Ohio National Guard, Fort Sumner,
Washington, D.C., June 13, 1864

"Went to the Capitol on Sunday to hear the Rev. Dr. Breckinridge of Kentucky—an uncle to the Rebel Genl. Breckinridge. The old man preached a very able sermon. He is 74 years of age and loyal as any man living, goes in for emancipation to its full extent.

"I see the nomination of Lincoln & Johnson is heartily endorsed all over the Country. We have a ratification meeting here tomorrow night—expect a large turn out should the weather continue fair."

– Charles M. Heaton, citizen,
Washington, D.C., June 14, 1864

"We had a great time here last night. The ratification meeting for Lincoln & Johnson was very large—the street between the Patent Office & Post Office was perfectly packed nearly the whole length of the Patent Office, & you know that covers two squares & the street & sidewalks are very wide. The fireworks was on the top of the building, and had the finest display of rockets & roman candles I ever seen. Some half dozen lighted balloons were sent up during the evening—no accident occurred at any time. I will send you the *Chronicle* containing an account of the meeting by the same mail that takes this."

– Charles M. Heaton, citizen,
Washington, D.C., June 16, 1864

"old father abe was here a few days a go [June 22, 1864], he came up [the James River] on his gun boat, and went up on the tower[156] of which I was speaking and was told by General Wetsel [Godfrey Weitzel] that we were hundred days men from ohio, and was quite astonished to know that we were so close to the front, the General said iff he had have known it too hours sooner we should have been sent to Norfolk, he also said we should not be sent into battle."

– William Budd Shinn, 138th Ohio National Guard, Spring Hill, Va., June 25, 1864

"I have always been a strong Republican and am still, but I declare, I do not know whether I can possibly muster courage enough to vote for Mr. Lincoln at the next election or not. I expect to deposit my vote for him but for only one reason, and that is that I consider it the only safe course for a Union man to take, in view of the immense pressure brought to bear by the 'Copperheads' and enemies of the country to defeat him. So much for politics."

– Surgeon Henry Hedge Mitchell, 36th US Colored Infantry, Boston, Mass., July 7, 1864

"the first thing you say you here we ar going to vollenteer for an other hundred days dont believe any such a thing I tell you planely as soon as my time is in I will be home dont Believe any thing you here at tall I woddent vollenteer another hundred days to save old Jonney Bruf[157] and old abe lincon Necks from the gallows that is the way I feel about vollenteering again so keep your sperritts yet time will soon be in every thing look quit [quiet] her But we dont [k]now any thing about what is going on a soldier is no more than a dog But it wont last long."

– William C. Barcus, 143rd Ohio National Guard, Wilson's Landing, Va., July 10, 1864

"We could go up to Fort Stevens when we pleased. . . . Pretty sharp skirmishing was going on when we got there. One great, nice dwelling in front of the fort was being burned to the ground. President Lincoln and lady were at the fort during the day and saw a part of the skirmishing. Rebel bullets are no respecter of persons.

His Excellency had to dodge one that came uncomfortably near his head. It wounded a surgeon standing close by him."

– Wilbur Fisk,[158] 2nd Vermont Infantry, Washington, D.C., diary entry for July 12, 1864

"a little before sundown the rebels made a charge on our men [at Fort Stevens] but they fired there large seige guns and the rebs were drove back with heavy loss such a noise it shook the very earth old Abe was in the fight some of the reb's sharp shooters were concealed in a house and they was shooting at him and he told our men to set it afire it was a house [that] cost several thousand dollars that was about dusk the flames shot upward and the conflagration illuminated the country for miles around they kept up their fireing untill after nine oclock when it graduly died away."

– Unidentified "Jake," 147th Ohio Infantry, Fort Ethan Allen, Washington, D.C., July 16, 1864

"tel your Father that all the Rebs we see want to know who is for President they all say they want McCleland to be elected but Old Abe suits the soldiers of this army and we will give him a large majority if they vote."

– Edgar Nicholas Shelden, 150th New York Infantry, near Atlanta, Ga., July 25, 1864

"The 'cops' [Copperheads] must still hear that they are below par. Philip Huber the Chief among them had a pretty severe treatment by some returned soldiers at Sinking Spring. They would have killed him if the citizens would not have interfered. It had a good effect for they say he intends voting for Lincoln."

– George W. Fraser, 195th Pennsylvania Infantry, Lincoln, Pa., July 29, 1864 "you wanted to know how the solgers will vote they all go in fore olde Abe and Jonson hole hog to they are a fiting harde to the front thare is a great many wounded going threw here evry day I wish the coper heds of the north was in my power it makes me so mad to see how they act."

– Charles C. Bark, 1st Ohio Light Artillery,
Bridgeport, Ala., July 30, 1864

"The army feel our late failures and are sadly disappointed. I fear unless Gen. Grant does a big thing soon, he will lose the friendship and confidence of the Potomac Army boys and Abraham too. Already we hear many saying they will never vote for old Abe, he will not be our next President, &c. &c. I dont know what the result will be, but I fear things will not go well the coming fall. There has been a wonderful change in the mind of the army within two weeks past. But we will continue to hope all will be well in the end."

– Thomas Edwards, 8th New York Heavy Artillery,
near Petersburg, Va., August 5, 1864

"just see how many valuable lives were lost only a few days ago, by the blundering of some one, and we do not know who it is, or we will never know how many lives were lost,[159] but Woe will be to them that send so many Souls to Eternity I hope Father we will never be called to witness another such slauter as this was, and then see what a story sombody got up, they said the Rebbels blew up one of our Forts, and as they charged we were ready to receive them with double shotted guns and they tryed to make us believe we killed three times as many of them, but I dont believe one word they say, my faith in Genl. Grant is gone, and if I now had 5000 votes, I would put them all in against old 'Abe the Butcher and niger worshiper' when two men are guilty of one and the same offence, one a niger, the other a white man, and the President hangs the white and pardons the black, I am against him, and that has been done by that old miser.[160] Father you must not vote for him again he is ruining our Country."

– Cornelius Van Houten,[161] 1st New Jersey Light Artillery, near Petersburg, Va., August 8, 1864

"you said that the rebs had played the old harry in Pennsylvania that they had burnt the half of Chamberburgh[162] that is nothing for them to do you aught to see the country that both of the armys has passed through we have drove the rebs one hundread miles and thare is nothing but one of brest works after another all the way and we have faught over ever[y] foot of the ground and I think that the war will close after the election that is if some one is put in besides old abe for thare is to much negro wool in him to stop the war."

– James P. Ramsey, 125th Ohio Infantry, camp near Atlanta, Ga., August 21, 1864

"As to the Presidential contest, if there really should be any, or if it should rise to the dignity of a contest, I cannot speak. I do not think the Butternuts & Copperheads can harmonize at Chicago,[163] but if they should, it is no matter. Old Abe can beat any nag they may trot out, out of his boots, and we are just letting him elect himself in this state, as we have other matters to attend to than fighting shadows, and the opposition has not even presented a shadow unless we count Freemont[164] as such, and if he has a single supporter in the state he has failed to make himself heard."

– James Hastings Drennen,[165] citizen, Martins Ferry, Ohio, August 22, 1864

"The Democratic Copperheads will make a terrible effort to defeat Mr. Lincoln but I dont think they can do it—in all the states but Indiana & Illinois the soldiers can vote in the field—but for those two states provision will be made as far as possible for them to go home to vote. In this way I think Mr. Lincolns election will be certain.

. . . It is our intention to get home Saturday evening the 8th Oct. for supper. I should like very much if we could get there in time for the fair, but we cannot do it—for I must so arrange my leave of absence so as to remain after the Nov. Election—the next day after the Nov. election we must start back."

– Charles M. Heaton, citizen,
Washington, D.C., August 23, 1864

"'Old Abe the Butcher' will not promote a good and loyal pravate but if he can find a man that will kill a white man and lift a nigger to Glory then that old Pirate will run him up anyhow,   for the North this war is played out   I see that a great portion of the people are against the administration,   I hope they will put that Old rail splitter in the first sink they can find,   he is the man that has killed or caused to be killed more good & brave men than this U.S. can ever boast of again,   through his power all this blood shed is come about. He thinks to much of the nigger,   it is a pity he hadent a wench and a coal black one too for a wife, and then he could have some of those mesigen[166] children the thing that he advocates so much   how he would like to see us soldiers mary niggers,   but I am running away with myself. I dont suppose you will be able to read one half of this letter for I am so mad I don't know what to do   I have suppo[sed] myself a Rebbel for awhile, and it is just so as I have writen,   I do not exagerate the thing at all. I say this war is no more to save the Union than Black soldiers are as good fighting men as white ones.

"Father I am very sorry to say I have no more faith in abe L—   he desires nothing but the advancement of the nigger and to fill his pockets. I believe he would sell our beloved country if he thought he could make himself rich by it. Father I hope you will not think I love my country the less now   if it was for my country and my country alone I was fighting. I would be willing to remain a private and fight all my life time, but as it has come now to a speculative business I must have some of the spoils or I will not stay. every

WHAT MISCEGENATION IS!

—AND—

WHAT WE ARE TO EXPECT

Now that Mr. Lincoln is Re-elected.

By L. SEAMAN, LL. D.

WALLER & WILLETTS, PUBLISHERS.

NEW YORK.

In 1864, Democrats in New York coined the term "miscegenation" to frighten voters into thinking that Republicans supported interracial marriage. This post-election pamphlet warned voters about "what we are to expect now that Mr. Lincoln is re-elected." (Lincoln Financial Foundation Collection, courtesy of the Allen County Public Library and the Indiana State Museum and Historic Sites) great tax that I am hardly able to keep my wife and I do not know what men does with three or four children. I shall use up more than my bounty twice over if things do not take a turn. I say I must have more wages if I am to fight for niggers and Abe L— or I will leave the first chance, for parts unknown. I will not stay here and see my family want for a thing—but as soon as they commence to fight for the union of states, and of hearts and not the Emancipation of slaves I will suffer all the hardship and go through any thing that it is in human nature to go through. I have allready sufferd and born the worst of hardships and am willing to bare more for my beloved country but not as I said before for the accursed negro. I would to God they might all sink and never be heard of for they and them alone have been the caus of all this war for if it had not been for the agitation of slavery all would have been well yet.

"I am very sorry to say Father that you are very much wrong when you say that McClellan has as many men as Grant he did not have much more than half, but then he would have done well enough with them if it hadent been for the administration. You say that Abe Lincoln is bound to enforce the laws against traitors, why dont he get them out of his midst, why dont he catch and hang those men all about Washington, there are thousands of men in and around Washington that he knows are not loyal and why dont he do his duty? but I have said enough for a letter, if I could talk to you I know I could convince you that you would be doing a great sin if you should vote for Abe again this faul. I have found out to much about him I am the one to experience all his misdeeds for it is the soldier that suffers by this war and Administration, he does not only suffer in the field, but he suffers while he sees his family that he loves more than all the world suffer for the commonest food."

– Cornelius Van Houten, 1st New Jersey Light Artillery,
Fort Warren, Va., August 25, 1864

"I think the authorities have used us very mean, as we never volunteered to serve as infantry and think they are not justifiable in expecting same from us. The government has hurt itself through red-taping its soldiers, and the boys do not have the confidence as heretofore. I think Old Abes days are numbered this election, although under the circumstances he has done all in his power to uphold the progress of the U. States. I hope this cruel war will be over in a short time. I am in hopes of a speedy peace, though only for the rebels to submit."

– Theodore W. Stauffer, 2nd Pennsylvania Heavy Artillery,
Bermuda Hundred, Va., August 28, 1864

"the excitmit is Great here a bout McCl and Chicago convention I dont think old *Abe* will stand any show at all I know he wont if the soldiers has any thing to do with the election."

– Alfred B. Cree, 22nd Iowa Infantry,
near Charles Town, W.V., September 2, 1864

"we Received the news of the Nomination of Gen Geo. B. McClullen the 3d of this month and there was great rejoising through the army the army will surely go for little Mac Gen Hancock[167] our corps commander made a Speach to the troops yesterday advising them to vote for Mac what do you think of that when the glourious Hancock one of our best generals and the Republicans one of the great lovers of the country come out for little Mac A Man who the Republicans say is a Traitor what do you think of that tell them to put that into there pipes and smoke it Mac will carry the army by an over whelming majority Every true and loyal man who Loves his country will vote for him And if he be elected peace will be once more restored to our bleeding Country but if he is defeated we know What to look for in the future as in the Past War for another four years untill every man in the north is killed or crippled I hope every candid man Will consider these things before he Votes and if Mac is elected there Will be great rejoising throught the country. . . . the Johnies are very quiet on our front and very friendly too We do not fire at each other while on Picket and we meet each other half Way between the line and exchange Coffe for Tobacco they say they are tired of the war but if Lincoln is elected They will fight another four years But if any other man be elected there Will be peace."

– Giles G. Berry, 17th Maine Infantry,
near Petersburg, Va., September 6, 1864

"The fall of Atlanta will give Lincoln fifty thousand votes. Richmond would elect him sure."

– Egbert Smith Woodworth, 171st Ohio Infantry,
Covington, Ky., September 7, 1864

"In regard to politics, it is my sincere belief that McClellan will be knocked higher than a kite next November. I do not think he will poll a very heavy vote in the army; the soldiers cannot swallow the Chicago platform[168] and his being nominated by such men as Vallandigham (whom every soldier hates like poison) and the Woods. I saw a man from Baltimore the other day, colonel of a Maryland (white) regiment, who says that Maryland will give a good majority for Lincoln, what do you think of that?"

– Charles E. Walbridge, 100th New York Infantry,
Bermuda Hundred, Va., September 11, 1864

"you need not to bee oneasy a bout the Draft for Abraham Lincoln will draft them if they dont want to go for they do us more harm at home then the southern solldiers does and thay half just as good a wright to fight for the goverment as I half and thay shall help us now."

– George W. Thompson, 21st Illinois Infantry,
Atlanta, Ga., September 13, 1864

In this Election Day scene, soldiers in the Army of the Potomac discuss politics and cast their ballots. Nineteen northern states passed legislation permitting soldiers to vote in the election. (Collection of Jonathan W. White)

"I will tell you that I have got over all sorts of patriotic feeling. The whole thing is a speculation from beginning to end. Old Abe has done what he could to keep the thing going till this fall and now he would like to do something merely because his election depends on something being done. He cant have my vote anyhow. If I cant do better than vote for him, I will not vote at all for I will never give my vote to inflict him upon the country for another four years. I believe his wife is a traitor and has more influence over him than is good for the country."

– George W. Cross, 10th New York Heavy Artillery,
Fort Craig, Arlington County, Va., September 18, 1864

"How encouraging every thing is looking of late and how our successes and the McClellan platform, and lastly the nomination of Seymour,[169] have changed the minds of our soldiers. A few weeks ago, Abraham had few friends. All were going to vote for 'Little

Mac.' Now we can hardly find one who dare say he will vote for him. Every one seems to think the reelection of Lincoln will nearly put an end to the rebellion, that if he is reelected, war will not last much longer. God grant it may be so."

– Thomas Edwards, 8th New York Heavy Artillery,
near Petersburg, Va., September 20, 1864

"Who do you think will be our next President? I would like to have power to appoint my man and that is *Old Abe*. I say let him finish this war. He can do it and he will do it if he is let alone. If Little Mac goes in for President and gets elected, there will be a compromise as sure as guns and if Abe is elected, he will keep this war going until every rebel is subdued and crushed or he will spill every drop of blood in the North. Therefore, he is my man. I say now we have commenced war, let us have war until one side or the other comes to an unconditional surrender. Let it be all North or all South. A compromise would be a disgrace to the North. We would be the laughing stock of the world."

– Marcus O. Thompson, 5th US Artillery,
Fort Hamilton, New York City, September 20, 1864

"How is Mclelland going to run at Home   do you think He will get many votes. He will not get a great maney in this armey, but still there are some Mclelland men, men who are tird of fighting and want Peace on any terms. We have got the Rebs on a part way now for bringing them back on our own terms. And I say elect Uncle Abe again and we will do It. The Rebs hate lincoln worse than any other man we could run. And that is the very reason why we should elect Him."

– James Alexander Stewart, 98th Ohio Infantry,
Atlanta, Ga., September 21, 1864

"Now you will do a great favour for me if you have me assessed and pay the Election fee for me.[170] I shall try and make it all right with you hereafter. I want to give Father Abraham a hoist and I want my vote to do some good. Our company will go in pretty strong for Lincoln although the principal part have voted the Democrat ticket heretofore."

– Francis W. Wallace, 147th Pennsylvania Infantry,
Atlanta, Ga., September 26, 1864

"Write me a long letter & tell me if you have been down to see the Dresden folks & how you are all going for Pres. I see you did nobly for Gov.[171] May the whole Union follow your lead & put Lincoln & Johnson in the chairs of state, that Rebels may howl & gnash their teeth for the tightening of Union measures & the downfall of their arrogant pride that 'Lincoln should never rule over them' &c."

– John Hawthorn, 9th Iowa Infantry,
East Point, Ga., September 26, 1864

"Times is hard hear fore pore folks every Thing is high Butt I Think That when old Abe Linken is alected again and our northern rebles is Beet Times will change The Darkes hour is Just Before day and wee hope The Time is near att hand when This un holy rebellion will Bee putt down and our union restord and The stares and stripes floate over us again."

– Henry C. Edgington,[172] citizen,
Scioto County, Ohio, October 2, 1864

"I begin to have more faith than ever in both Genl. Grant and President Lincoln too. I do believe that Uncle Abe has done all in his power to preserve the Union in its purity. I am very sorry I ever denounced him as I did because I now truly believe he is worthy to be our President, and I farther believe that the Chicago Convention was a regular Secesh concern, and they thought more about helping the Rebels than they did about the preservation of our Union.

"Father I have come over to your views of the case. I now truly believe that no honorable peace can be had without fighting for it, for if the McClellan platform was carried out we surely never would have our Union as it was, or we never could have a thorough peace as long as he was in Offace. Father I am now a real true Lincolnite. I will stand up for him and the Administration as long as I have two legs, and I am willing to fight now till we restore our loved Union or are prostrated. I under stand now just how things are working There is a cirtain class of men who would do almost anything if they could only see a southern Confederacy, but it shall not be. Grant is doing big work now, but I suppose you know the news before I do."

– Cornelius Van Houten, 1st New Jersey Light Artillery,
camp about eight miles from City Point, Va., October 3, 1864

"Philadelphia's great heart beat high with patriotism last night. A great political, or rather *Union* demonstration was made in the shape of a grand torch light procession. I think there must have been at *least* 15,000 torch bearers and perhaps 20,000. The display was the finest I have ever seen of the kind. Such gatherings please me very much for they show *plainly* which way the '*Union* wind blows'; they show the determination of the American people *never* to bow their heads under the yoke of treason. The whole city was alive with enthusiasm. All along the line of march, miles in length, the air was continually rent with cheers for Union and our noble old President, while from a score of bands could be heard, 'The Battle Cry of Freedom, The Star Spangled Banner,' & other such patriot-soul-stirring airs. Everybody was there. Biddy and Paddy stood upon the sidewalk & '*hoorayed*' for 'Ould Abe.' Dinah looked out from the kitchen window pleased and astonished. Nellie, the Chestnut St. belle, waved her embroidered handkerchief from the doorway, while her jewels sparkled in the dazzling light, & Grandame was looking out with her specs. His honor, the Alderman was present, and Billy, the bootblack, was there. All classes, all trades, were represented. Here limped a convalescent soldier grasping his lamp, and there stalked a millionaire proudly along, *all* delighted to honor the people's candidate 'Honest Old Abe.'"

– Lawrence Johnson, 9th New York Heavy Artillery, Satterlee Hospital, Philadelphia, Pa., October 9, 1864

"they have some warm times out here this state goes for Old Abe there is some copperheads peace at any price men here but they are few and as a general thing cant either read or write but they are crazy for Mclellan I dont beleive they know the difference between the two platforms one offered to bet fifty cts with Wib to night that Mclelan would be elected Wilber offered to bet him fifty dollars that he would not he didnot want to bet more than he was worth but he owned up that he honestly thought Lincoln would be the next president."

– Electa (Young) Jolls, citizen, Waterloo, Iowa, October 11, 1864

"We may remain here or hereabouts until Lincoln is re-elected, in view of the fact that the rebels will surely do something perfectly *desperate* in order to assist McClellan. It is even possible that they may load *their whole army* with eight or ten days rations, leave Richmond to its fate, & march with superhuman speed on *Washington*. . . . You cant think how much the army looks upon the *election* as decisive of the war. In some regiments there is not a single man who will vote for McClellan, some regiments have two or three McClellanites, but I *know* that fully 9/10 of the army vote will be for Lincoln. Lest I should get the figure too high I will say 4/5—but we shall *see*. If the rebel army were to vote, every *real* rebel among them would vote for G. B. McClellan. I have talked with several of the women in the valley as I passed their houses and their *most anxious* question was whether Lincoln or McClellan was probably going to be President."

– Theodore Frelinghuysen Vaill, 2nd Connecticut Heavy Artillery, Front Royal, Va., October 11, 1864

"Maj. Waters has been at our Regt. and taken their votes. The Regiment went almost wholly for '*Old Abe*' as most sensible people do. There was some deserters came into our camp the other day from the Rebs and they said—if Lincon was elected they would have but little hope, and it would be a hard matter to get many of them to fight any more. The coming Election is looked to with a hope of its having some thing of an influence for the better, and such we think will be the case, but of course we cannot tell."

– Alburtus H. Peckham, 185th New York Infantry,
near Petersburg, Va., October 18, 1864

"I put in a vote for Old Abe the other day. I thought it was my duty to do so. I could not vote for McClellan on the Chicago platform. I could not vote for a man that the Rebs would cheer for. They have done it & say if he is elected they will have their rights, & I dont know what rights they want unless it is Secession. They have had every other right offered them."

– Merritt Pierce, 1st New York Engineers,
camp near Chaffin's Bluff, Va., October 19, 1864

Soldiers from Pennsylvania cast their ballots in this scene in camp. (Collection of Jonathan W. White)

"well I gess I will *tell* you a little about how I am getting along we got orders last Friday to start for City Point but did not start till Saturday noon when we was ordered to fall in with evry thing on namely knapsack with my clothing blanket & evry thing amost in & over coat straped on top haversack canteen gun catriage Box with 40 rounds of amunition in quite a load after standing about one half an hour we marched up to the white house whare Old Abe come out to see us & after talking to us a few minutes we marched down to the wharf & got aboard a steamer tired eneoagh having marched about 4 miles besides standing with all on."

– Norman Orlando Wheeler, 189th New York Infantry,
City Point, Va., October 25, 1864

"You wanted to know what I ment by Father's putting in my vote,[173] has he not received my vote which I sent home some time ago & which fully explains on the out side of the Envelop what is to be done with it. I suppose Father is a going to vote for little

This anti-McClellan cartoon, "The Gunboat Candidate at the Battle of Malvern Hill," depicts the Democratic nominee as an incompetent military leader as he sits in a saddle astride the Union ironclad *Galena* during the failed Peninsula Campaign of 1862. (Library of Congress)

McCllel is he not or is he for honest old abe Lincoln & not the Copperhead Mcllelan or in other words Gun Boat McClelan[174] he thought he had a firm Platform, but how sadly mystake[n] he was when one of Grants shells burst underneath it & Blew it into attoms. if I vote for McClellan I vote for Pendilton[175] & before I cast a vote for either I would cut my right arm off. I might just as well vote for Jeferson davis as them Peace men. I am for Peace just as much as any man living, but I want it on honorable terms (Unconditional Surrender) & their Rebel leader dwelt [dealt] with according to the laws of the U.S."

– Charles C. Miller, 140th New York Infantry,
near Petersburg, Va., October 30, 1864

"I supose that you are all thinking about who will be our next President I will tell you Lincoln of course we want a union man we are not makeing a president for the South but for the Nort[h] then let us as a Company vote for Lincoln and have our wrights or fight fore years more we cant loose all that we have gained nor we shant."

– Charles A. Lamos, 1st Vermont Heavy Artillery,
Strasburg, Va., November 4, 1864

"In the Union at large we hope that no laggard soldier and stupid politician with a double dyed traitor for his right bower[176] will be elected President and bring back to the army (if there is an army) all the Buells[177] and Porters[178] who for two years *wasted* the blood and treasure of a brave but longsuffering people. The 16th, thank Heaven, is all right. Our vote stood 379 for Lincoln to 13 for McClellan. No other regiment in this brigade can show so good a record. The '60th' gave about 60 majority for Lincoln."

– Noble L. Prentiss, 16th Illinois Infantry,
Kingston, Ga., November 7, 1864

"i wish pet that you would let me know, how montvill goes and how conn[ecticut] goes in perticular for i am in hopes it will go for Little Mc but it is all over now either Lincoln is reelected or Mc is and i hope the latter for i dont want to stay out here two years more. and i think that if old Abe is reelected i had better inlist in the regular army for they are giving eighteen hundred dollars to men to enlist in the regulars for five years."

– Chester Alphonso Chapman, 1st Connecticut Heavy Artillery, Bermuda Hundred, Va., November 6, 1864

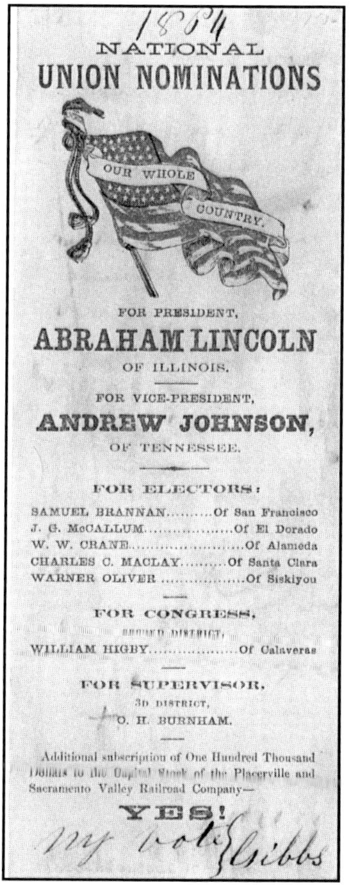

1864

NATIONAL

UNION NOMINATIONS

OUR WHOLE COUNTRY.

FOR PRESIDENT,

ABRAHAM LINCOLN

OF ILLINOIS.

FOR VICE-PRESIDENT,

ANDREW JOHNSON,

OF TENNESSEE.

FOR ELECTORS:

SAMUEL BRANNAN..........Of San Francisco
J. G. McCALLUM..................Of El Dorado
W. W. CRANE.........................Of Alameda
CHARLES C. MACLAY.........Of Santa Clara
WARNER OLIVER ....Of Siskiyou

FOR CONGRESS,

[illegible] DISTRICT,

WILLIAM HIGBY..................Of Calaveras

FOR SUPERVISOR,

3D DISTRICT,

O. H. BURNHAM.

Additional subscription of One Hundred Thousand Dollars to the Capital Stock of the Placerville and Sacramento Valley Railroad Company—

YES!

my vote Gibbs

A "National Union" ballot from California. (Lincoln Financial Foundation Collection, courtesy of the Allen County Public Library and the Indiana State Museum and Historic Sites)

"Today is the great election—one of the most important ever held on the country comes off today and the result will be felt for a long time to come. I have no doubt that Abraham Lincoln will be elected. I do not think Gen. McClellan is to be trusted. The 88th [Illinois] went on to the works and relieved the 125th Ohio while they went in to vote. The Illinois boys could not vote because the Copperhead Legislature were afraid to trust them and well they might for shame on a body who will disenfranchise men because they are fighting for their country."

– Lt. George W. Kent, 88th Illinois Infantry, Chattanooga, Tenn., diary entry for November 8, 1864

"To day is the great day of Days up North which is to decide whether the Patriot and Statesman Abraham Lincoln is to be president or whether the Humbug General McLellan is to disgrace this great nation by assuming the reins of Government March next. I have little or no fear about the result although Illinois going for McLellan would not surprise me very much. Could her brave boys in Blue vote there would be no doubt as to the result as a vote taken in our Regiment well shows. We had 410 men and officers present for duty and of these McLellan got 19 votes, Lincoln 391. Co D gave an unanimous 46 votes for Lincoln not a traitor in it, every one True Blue. I feel proud of them. Proud that their record has gone on to Gov Yates[179] in that way, for the vote was taken at the instigation of Gov Yates that he might know how his boys stood even if the infernal villains at home did vote him and his party down. The 2nd and 7th Iowas are voting to day, their state not being afraid to let their soldiers vote although absent on the tented field. A curse ever on the infernal Copps of Illinois who would not let us vote because we went forth to fight their Battles and let them stay at home."

– Capt. Don Carlos Newton, 52nd Illinois Infantry,
Rome, Ga., November 8, 1864

"For this last two months an expression of anxiety has marked the countenances of all supporters of the present national administration, but the work of yesterday has dispelled the gloom, and a radiant joy beams from the face of every true Union man to day. A great burden has been removed, the Presidential election is past and that too without more than the usual amount of excitement. Lincoln is reelected, Freedom is secured, and the government is saved. In my humble opinion, from this day dates the rapid decline of the hell begotten rebellion which has caused so much bloodshed and destruction for the last 3½ yrs, and has well nigh destroyed our very nationality. Thank God for our present happy prospects, and trust in our rulers to soon establish us as a nation, the most enviable upon the face of the earth, not merely a Republic in theory, but so in reality."

– George Eastburn,[180] student, Yale College,
New Haven, Conn., November 9, 1864

"I suppose Old Abe [is] elected again,   you spok about Charley voting for him,   he is not old enough to vote but I guess if he had been, he would,   when he left home he was a strong McClellan man, but he is straddle of the fence ready to fall the way the largest crowd goes   I stand firm yet & think I allways shall,   I know I as long as this war last[s] for I long for peace,   give me peace rather than war   we have had war enough for the last four years, but their is a fair prospect for four years more if Abe is electid   but I only enlisted for one year & let them get me any longer if they can, if I live that length [of] time."

– Ira Brown, 188th New York Infantry,
camp near City Point, Va., November 12, 1864

"The overwhelming majority which 'old Abe' has received is the worst blow the rebs have yet received, and as soon as they see this they will conclude that a *united North* is against them and all hopes of compromise, and all questions of peace, are settled, except upon *our* terms. The result of this election to the rebs has inflicted upon them *more* damage than the capture of *2* Richmonds would. I tell you Johny that there is *no* way in which to bring them to terms except to *whip* them and I trust with the faithful leaders we now have this will soon be accomplished and all enemys of our country, both South & North, will be on their knees pleading forgiveness. The mass of the people South desire peace, and *on our* terms also, but the damnable leaders are the men which we have got to *subjugate*. Those men once in our power, and [the] Southern confederacy will be but a bubble."

– Sumner Hill,[181] citizen, Salem, Mass., November 14, 1864

"I did not get my business settled at Washington the clerks had gone home on furlough I may be able to do it by writing of course I did not get my pay I saw honest Abe, and he looked as though he expected to be elected again how is it, do you think he is elected sure."

– Dr. Peres S. Randall,[182] veteran, Maysville, Ky., November 15, 1864

"To change the subject, I must relate my trip and experience in Detroit the other day [Tuesday, November 1], or rather it was more than a week ago. I had resolved to serve Old Abe one day at least as I could not have the pleasure of voting for father Abraham.

"It was announced in the *Bill* that on Tuesday at Detroit, Sec. Chase, Dan. S. Dickinson, Fred Hausurek,[183] [Rev. Maxwell P.] Gaddis [of Cincinnati], [Michigan governor Austin] Blair, and others would enlighten the people on the great questions of the hour. The day was as gay as sunshine and a pure bracing air could make it. The city had chartered some cars to take the Ann Arbor delegation to Detroit. We had the band ready and in due time the train from Chicago arrived. The band saluted the crowded train, and our three empty coaches were unlocked and we were soon all aboard for Detroit. We had a fine trip down and marched with the band up into the city to the 'Wigwam,' an enormous building, rough and capacious, for the accommodation of the great political meetings. We were informed that we would all be furnished with torchlights at six in the evening. With three cheers for Lincoln, we scattered for the 'every where.'"

– Levi Jay Brown,[184] student,
University of Michigan, November 20, 1864

"who Did he vote for old abe or little Piss Pot—they say or the Paper ses that old abe has sent men to Richmond to see what they can Do on the Peace question I Dont think we can have Peace untill we Run the Rebs all in to hell or some other good Place they wont give up as long as they have got a man to fight."

– John March, 23rd New York Infantry,
Harpers Ferry, W.V., November 21, 1864

"When I was at home I had Gay and hapy times but they are played out now, but their may be a better day coming. I think that was al write making that flow [fellow?] sing, but praying I dont think would have done much good for his Country or old abe, for the prarys of the wicked availeth nothing."

– John M. Lain, 3rd Iowa Cavalry,
Memphis, Tenn., December 6, 1864

"Old Abe's speech[185] was an able one—well written—but poorly pointed. His administration has developed more dishonest men than the whole Republic ever did & who will care for his neighbor or Brother when his government collaterals are safe from seizure. But enough of war. I do not mean to have one word on politics when I get home."

– Thomas William Hendee,[186] citizen,
Hull, England, December 31, 1864

Lt. Gen. Ulysses S. Grant at his headquarters in Cold Harbor, Va., June 1864. (Library of Congress)

1865

"the march that day was an easy one of 11 miles got into camp early and the boys went out for fresh pork and chickens I got an excellent supper at one farm house for 25 cents, the old lady of the house had a queer idea of the war, she clamed that if some one of the rebel army would kill Jeff Davis and some one of the Yankey army will kill Linkoln why then she though[t] there would be nobody to set men to fighting."

– Robert Neville, 103rd Ohio Infantry,
Waynesboro, Tenn., January 6, 1865

"I believe Grant is all right and will prove himself to be one of the Greatest Generals of this world, he and Abraham Lincoln are just the men we have wanted this long while God has raised them both for this especial purpose, bothe are of but common birth, and it will be sufficien[t] to immortalize them bothe if they bring about a Union once again, each man is in his place now Faragot [Admiral David G. Farragut] on the sea, Grant on the land and Lincoln at the head of our nation. I think the people are becoming more sencable [sensible] every day."

– Cornelius Van Houten, 1st New Jersey Light Artillery,
camp near Petersburg, Va., January 9, 1865

"Shall I write you a little about the celebrities of Washington and their doings? If so, here goes: New Year's day (Jany 2), the President of the United States had a reception, according to custom. I was there and shook the hands of our *graceful* Chief Magistrate, wished him a Happy New Year, to which he replied in a few kind words,—and came away with the prayer in my heart, '*Long* live Uncle Abe!' Last night he had another reception, but I had a prior engagement and couldn't honor him with my presence. Last Wednesday night, Mr. Lincoln and wife were at the Theatre, and I walked out close by them, and had a good long look at their various points of beauty. The conclusion there arrived at was this: They are both better looking than their pictures, especially Mrs. Lincoln. I do not call the President a bad-looking man, and think Mrs. L. decidedly good-looking. 'Our honored Chief Magistrate' has a sad, despairing expression of countenance, which almost tempts you to cry. Any one that sees him cannot help feeling a sympathy and regard towards him. That at least was my experience, and others speak in a similar strain.

"I have also seen Vice-Admiral Farragut and wife, Secretary Stanton and wife, Gens. [Winfield Scott] Hancock, [Montgomery] Meigs, [George Armstrong] Custer, [Silas] Casey, nearly all the Senators and Representatives in Congress, and many other eminent men. But the greatest of them all, to *my* mind, is *Edwin Forrest*, the great tragedian, who is now acting at Fords Theatre. There is something sublime and most wonderful in that man's power. He hasn't his equal on the stage in Europe or America. . . .

"I was in Congress twice last week and heard speeches from various gentlemen both of the Senate and the House, among which was [Glenni William] Scofield's reply to [James] Brooks speech, and the witty crushing reply of Brooks. This Brooks is *James* of the *New York Express*, and in my opinion the best speaker in the House. I do not approve of the principles of the Copperheads, but I cannot help admiring the eloquence of some of their champions.

"The best speaker in the Senate, to my mind, is Lyman Trumbull of Illinois, a scholarly, logical man, whose every word and gesture counts. Chas. Sumner [of Massachusetts] can do the 'heavy' eloquence better but is not so ready and sharp and penetrating as Trumbull."

– John Deering Jr.,[187] Second Auditor's Office,
Treasury Department, Washington, D.C., January 10, 1865

"I think if old abe would come and see some [of] the battle fields he would quit issueing so many niger proclamation[s] but all his talk is nothing but niger."

– Kramer Gabler, 140th Pennsylvania Infantry,
near Petersburg, Va., January 27, 1865

"It is reported that Vice President Stephens[188] of the Southern Confederacy is here negotiating terms of peace but I cannot believe it until I see him. I should think the Rebs would begin to feel like coming to terms on our conditions for they are losing ground now very fast and they must know their cause is hopeless; they are like a great many *girls*, or *young ladies*, whom we know; see they are wrong but too proud to acknowledge they are *in fault*. What great rejoicing there would be if it was made known that Alexander Stephens had come here to accept of the terms which Abraham Lincoln considers to be right. I am willing to let Uncle Abe decide upon what we shall give them and what we shall not."

– John H. Stevens, 151st New York Infantry,
Washington, D.C., February 1, 1865

"I say restore the Union with the Abolition of Slavery for there has been too much Loyal Blood shed on our side to give up the contest now with disgrace to us. Slavery has always been a curse to the Country and let us hope that when the Union is restored, there will be no bondmen in the land. The reelection of President Lincoln has been a crushing blow to the South, and they feel it deeply too. But it is a victory on our side that all good Union men rejoice at, and none more so than the soldiers of this army. McClellan was once a great General and I was once proud to say that I was a soldier in his army. But he chose bad company and his star has shone and burnt out. So as he makes his path, let him walk it."

– William A. White, 82nd Pennsylvania Infantry,
near Petersburg, Va., February 14, 1865

"We are closing in on the rebs on all sides. [George H.] Thomas, Grant, and others with their armies will make a peace that will last. I feel glad that old Abe is going to fight it out. The soldiers never were more determined or more confident of success. Nearly all go in for fighting it out. As for myself, I never had a doubt but we would be successful. All that we have to do is stick to it and we'll surely conquer."

– Benjamin Franklin Blatchford, 2nd Massachusetts Heavy
Artillery, Federal Point, N.C., February 16, 1865

"Lincolns Inaugural, while the sentiments are noble, is one of the most awkwardly expressed documents I ever read—if it be correctly printed. When he knew it would be read by millions all over the world, why under the heavens did he not make it a little more creditable to American *scholarship*?"

– Rev. Arthur B. Bradford,[189] citizen,
Enon Valley, Pa., March 8, 1865

"I would say this much to brother Solomon. If he sees any possible escape of the Draft, that he shall take the advantage of it; for my part I would rather prefer 10 years among entire strangers than to fight one year for old Abe and the freedom of the niggers, it is very little that I will do if I can help it."

– Jacob D. Row, 17th Indiana Infantry,
Nashville, Tenn., March 8, 1865

"Yesterday, Sunday, the 26th inst, the entire armies of the James were reviewed by old abe Lincoln, and he rode along the lines with his hat off, and such cheering, and playing of national airs by the bands, I never shall forget."

– Henry Clay Ridgway, 199th New York Infantry,
camp near City Point, Va., March 27, 1865

"We were marched (our 5 Corps) near the scene of action in heavy marching order—that is, all our traps on our backs, and in the afternoon, passed review before our President Abraham Lincoln. I liked the appearance of him first rate and he is by no means such [a] humbly [homely?] fellow as thee picture him. I marched within 4 roads [rods?] of him and took a pretty fair look at him. He was on horseback of course. After review we went closer to the battle ground but did not come in fire, we are in reserve at present, and have to go wherever we are needed along the whole line. We are in camp again, but are ready to march on a moments notice. I do not anticipate any great danger now. The Johnnys got a severe lesson, but i cannot say how many thee [they?] lost. There are so many different yarns about it. Our boys give em fits it is sayd. What Lincoln and the ladys thought when thee [they] reviewed us, under the thunder of cannons and roar of musketry, i guess was this, poor Fellows how many of you will lay low before long. I have no doubt, there was the human feeling touched, especially as one of our companynie right in front of the President while we were marching along under our torn and tattered colleurs,[190] broke rank and knelt right before the lady[s] coach. He is half witted only, or light headed."

– Louis F. DuPless, 6th Wisconsin Infantry,
Petersburg, Va., March 27, 1865

"Just as we had finished dinner today some one came in & said Lincon was coming down Grace Street. We had heard the guns fired, in honor of his arrival, & we went to the window to see him, as one would go to look at a wild beast. He & his son & four officers were in an ambulance drawn by four splendid horses, then came a carriage with four more officers & then about thirty men on horse back. . . . The streets were *crowded*, mostly tho with negroes, & they [were] *huzzaring & hollowing*. One said, 'Jeff Davis did not wait to see his master but he had come at last.' He was gallanted [gallivanted?] to the Presidents house where he now remains."

– Frances Anne (Sutton) Doswell,[191]
Richmond, Va., diary entry for April 4, 1865

"I hope the President will keep out of danger; the *Chivalry* are a greater set of scoundrels than he thinks them to be. Mr. Lincoln's personal safety is of such vast importance to the country at this time, that his friends feel more or less solicitude when they read of his 'going to the front.' But he has made a glorious trip this time."

– William H. Hanna,[192] citizen,
Bloomington, Ill., April 4, 1865

"Mr Jeff. Davis. I dont heer any thing from him any more I think he is a very unmanerly Gentleman for Uncle Abe went down to see him and he was not at home. I would think Lincoln would feel good now four years ago he could not travel from Washington to Harrisburg Pa without disguise and now he can go right into their Capital and sleep if he likes in Jeff['s] own House. But I suppose they [there] are some men up north that yet hold to the doctrine that we can never subdue them. I dont know as we can but we can drive them out of the United States and that is all we want, 'to get rid of them.['] The People around here had quite a time Friday Evening There was a grand illuminations the fire Companies Paraded and the people listened to speaches delivered by some of the leading citizens—our office was decorated splended I wish you could of seen it there was a light to every pane of Glass and 3 Flags out of every window besides 2 large one[s] over the door Besides the Flags we had 24 paper Balloons made of red white and Blue Paper out of the windows But we had fun the next morning to clean up the candle greease. But that did not trouble us any for it was in a good cause that the grease got there and so it had to come off."

– Sylvester Rounds, Veteran Reserve Corps,
Trenton, N.J., April 9, 1865

"Well now I want to tell you what I suppose you know before this time. Richmond has fallen at last, and old Abe is occupying Jeff Davis' house. Did you rejoice any when you heard the news? All the Union people here illuminated their houses but the cops [Copperheads] put down their blinds."

– David Spielman,[193] citizen,
Blandinsville, Ill., April 10, 1865

"I addressed the meeting at some length, and with great care to myself, and apparent enthusiasm of the people.[194] The house was densely crowded, and a great mass out of doors. In the midst of my speech, about ten o'clock,[195] without apparent cause I had a sharp pain through my heart—just one pang, like the thrust of a sword—I shall bear sad news: some catastrophe has occurred. I spoke of it to several who had remarked my sudden paleness. Miss Bauken, a young, bright school teacher, told me, that as I stood perfectly calm, speaking with the banners in the back ground I looked like the pictures of Gen. Washington!"

– Elizabeth Oakes Smith,[196] citizen,
Patchogue, Long Island, N.Y., diary entry for April 14, 1865

"The whole country is in a whirl of excitement—President Lincoln was shot in the Theatre last night about ten o'clock. Secretary Seward also was attacked, and his two sons. The scene at the Theatre, terrible as it was—has in it the elements of the sublime. The Assassin must have been wrought up to a pitch of frenzy. He shot the President through the back of the head—six[197] persons being in the box at the time—he threw off an officer who caught him by the arm, sprang to the front of the box brandishing a dagger above his head, and cried in a loud voice *sic semper tyrannis*, leapt to the stage, ten feet beneath him, scattering the actors right and left, and then disappeared in the passages at the back of the theatre. Great God! how like a minister of vengeance he must have looked.

"Poor Lincoln! the tool and victim of party! seems hardly dealt with—vain and weak, and low-bred as he was, he was better than his party and the country will be the worse for his death."

– Elizabeth Oakes Smith,[198] citizen,
Patchogue, Long Island, N.Y., diary entry for April 15, 1865

"At 3 A.M. [upon hearing of Lincoln's assassination] a large number of men enlisted under several officers for the ostensible purpose of going in and burning the Old Capitol Prison and slaughtering the prisoners there confined.[199] For some reason they did not go.

"There is quite a feeling among the soldiers toward these Rebel deserters. They appear to have a great dislike for them.

"As the Presidents carriage was leaving the White House last night, the Presidents little boy [Tad] (some 12 years) came out in his night clothes and endeavored to go with the carriage saying that if his 'Father was Dead, he was going to see him.'

"The family of President Lincoln is no better nor was Lincoln any better to his family than one hundred thousand other husbands and Fathers killed during this War. It is his loss to his country and not to his family.

"No cars have passed between here and Baltimore to day, but now [at] 9 P.M. they are running again. Almost every house in Washington City is dressed in mourning. To-morrow we are expecting that *one gun in every half hour* will be fired during the day. This is the salute prescribed by the Regulations."

– Aurestus Sidney Perham, 23rd Maine Infantry,
Camp Berry, Washington, D.C., April 15, 1865

The Old Capitol Prison, which sat on the current site of the US Supreme Court, served as the meeting place for Congress following the burning of Washington, D.C., in 1814. During the Civil War it housed political prisoners and Confederate prisoners of war. (Library of Congress)

"Reports have come (I do not know whether Official or not) that Mr. Lincoln is not dead but that his wound is a very dangerous one. I hope he may live to pass sentence on his would be murderers. He is a good man and I believe has done what he could for the good of his Country."

– John M. Lovejoy, 121st New York Infantry,
near Burkes Junction, Va., April 15, 1865

"Joy unspeakable is in this moment turned to deepest mourning. The national heart has for some time been aroused to its highest pitch of excitement in rejoicing over the glorious success of our national arms, the establishment of peace, and the supremacy of our national emblems, but in one moment sorrow hath come to our jubilant people as fast as the wings of lightning can carry the sad news. Abraham Lincoln—our President, he whom the nation felt proud (in view of his admirable capacity and undying devotion to the cause of our country) to bestow upon him the highest honors of our nation, is murdered by an assassin. Who can describe the infamy of the atrocious act? Also Sect. Seward by the same assassinating plot is mortally wounded in this infamous act. He whose very life has become distinguished for his acts of kindness and mercy is murdered by one that has been an object of his benevolence. Is there a place in the 'blackness of darkness' deep enough for such a perpetrator?"

– Enoch Leavitt, 2nd Ohio Cavalry,
Baltimore, Md., April 15, 1865

"I suppose you have heard about the President's being shot before this. It is so dreadful—just when peace is dawning. But if he had been to church instead of a theatre, it might not have been."

– Sarah Goodrich,[200] citizen, Owego, N.Y., April 16, 1865

"I went down to the point and thear was a Lot of Leas [Robert E. Lee's] men thear they told me they was glad he [Lincoln] was dead if i had had a pistol, I would of put a ball thrue his hart *dam* him they Say they wil kil more blew beles[201] before this is over he ought to be strang up til he blowes away."

– Amasa Stanhope, 1st District of Columbia Cavalry,
City Point, Va., April 16, 1865

"libby I have some rather Bad news to tell you of which I supose you have herd of ere this that is of the deth of our President Abraham Lincoln it is a sad afair and has made many a sad heart for it seemed as if he was almost a Father to us after four years of hard service and then had to be assassinated in cold Blood it is to Bad I herd to Day that they had caught the man that shot him[202] I hope they have."

– Samuel A. Miller, 123rd Ohio Infantry,
Gallipolis, Ohio, April 16, 1865

"last night we received news by mail that cast a gloom over every joyous face Abraham Lincon President of the United States is ded Basely murdered by a cowardly foe. He who was doing his best to preserve a nation extending the olive branch of peece to a treachorous & traitorous[203] foe. They have fulfilled their threat that the war would not end under Lincons adminastration. The sacrifise of his life seems to me a needless dooings, one that will result to no good to them. And I think will not materily effect the Nations existence News like that flies on lightning wings. He died in Washington at 7.15 AM. By 7. PM we heard of it in Liberty Village. Seward[204] it is hoped will recover as will his sons."

– Hezekiah Banks Clements, staff of Gen. C. H. Van Wyck,
Liberty, N.Y., April 16, 1865

"The excitement occasioned by the terrible news of yesterday has not yet entirely subsided and therefore it is difficult for me to keep my thoughts together long enough to get them upon paper. Abraham Lincoln is no more!

"No longer ago than day before yesterday the people here were all elated at the glorious prospects before them. Recruiting to be stopped and the expenses reduced. Surely the end was drawing nigh. All were gay and joy gleamed from every countenance. All were congratulating each other that this cruel war was over. What a contrast was yesterday, a fearful gloom overshadowing every countenance, while the doleful gun, the tolling bell, and the city draped in mourning told of the terrible bereavement which the Nation had been doomed to suffer. The greatest and noblest of men, the national Chief Magistrate, had been stretched upon a bloody bier by the hand of a skulking assassin. Citizens looked each other in the face in blank astonishment, while deep in their eyes was a troubled look that bespoke of sorrow mingled with terrible vengeance.

"Last summer while I was at Washington I twice visited Ford Theatre. Once while there in the very midst of a play the stage manager came forward and said, 'Ladies & Gentlemen, Official intelligence has just been received that Atlanta is ours. Gen. Shermans forces entered it at three o'clock this morning,' and he added with a triumphant air, 'you can see what a man can do that gets up in the morning.' The applause was loud and long. Every loyal heart was full and every loyal mouth was open. The audience nearly all arose to their feet, hats and handkerchiefs were waved, and cheer after cheer was lustily given. The old Theatre resounded with the welcome of good news. The tumult would subside at times seemingly to be renewed again with greater vigor. When the joy had spent itself silence again resumed its sway and the play proceeded. While sitting there that night enjoying the good news and the Theatre, how little did I think of the awful, great, real tragedy so soon to be enacted there. I looked at the private boxes well, I remember they were filled with military personages, and the stars upon their shoulder straps told that they ranked of the first order. Abraham Lincoln was not there and it would have perhaps been well for him if he had never have gone there; and yet not there alone was he exposed to the assassin's bullets. Always about six o'clock in the evening he would leave the Executive Mansion for his cottage in the suburb of the city. On that occasion he always had a body guard, and there were always from ten to twenty curiosity seekers there eager to see him take his departure. Any man with nerves steady and strong enough to take unerring aim could easily have sent the deadly bullet on its awful mission then. And I thought to myself, that by taking the precaution to become acquainted with the grounds, and have a secure hiding place looked out in case that he should effect his escape, he could stand half a chance to get away even though he did the deed before the very face and eyes of a body guard of fifty men all mounted and armed to the teeth.

"The southern people must have been actuated by a blind and bigoted vengeance to have plotted such a scheme as the one which they have carried into execution. They know not what is for their own good and they care less. They have killed a great and noble man, one whose bosom was incapable of harboring a single revengeful feeling, one who though he has been stern and unceasing in his endeavors to crush the rebels, has always held the olive-branch to their view, and who has declared to them that if they would lay down their arms, he would exercise 'justice tempered with mercy.'

"Who will pardon Jeff Davis now? Aye, the bullet that layed Abraham Lincoln low killed the southerners best friend and roused a longing for revenge in northern men that one generation cannot clear away."

– Benjamin W. Briggs,[205] citizen,
Bloomington, Ill., April 16, 1865

Ford's Theatre. (Library of Congress)

"last night we had the sad inteligence that President Linclon, and secrtary seward ware assinated on the night of Apr 14". I can tell you I never since I have been in the Armey seen such a shaddow cast over our Regt as the [one] that news caused."

– Alonzo David Pierce, 6th Illinois Cavalry,
Eastport, Miss., April 17, 1865

"Well, I cannot overcome the awful murder of Lincoln. The people seem to be crazy with excitement and anger. *I do not* know how I feel in regard to his assassination. On Saturday, I thought it a false rumor, but afterwards was compelled to believe the terrible fact. Those who are willfully prejudiced say that he has been murdered by the Democratic Party, a plot long premeditated by the *Knights* of the Golden Circle.[206] Indeed, I feel *very* sorry that such a wicked crime should be committed as much as anyone, but when we are slurred and told of it as being members, and entertaining the same feelings that the assassin did, tis not pleasant and has a tendency to irritate and change the mind."

– Laura J. Morgan,[207] citizen, Sunbury, Pa., April 18, 1865

"My heart is nigh to bursting and my eyes are swimming in tears. Our Countrys Protector and best friend is no more. Murdered by a *Fiend, a Devil.* Was there ever any thing so horrid before? But I cannot write about it, for you know it all as well as we. And as He was your neighbor and friend I know you will mourn in sadness at *his* great loss. But sister, his work is done and our Heavenly Father has taken him home, and when I read the piece you sent in your letter about his needing rest I thought, Now he has rest eternal. No more cares, no more anxiety, no more sorrow or pain, all is over and he is at *rest.*

"But Sister, I must tell you how I have felt for the past year about him. I have seen such a true semblance between him and Moses and have been so afraid he would not be permitted to see the Canaan, for you know Moses got in sight of the promised land but was not permitted to enter it, that I felt afraid our President would be murdered at or about the time of his second Inauguration, and when he went to Richmond I was very anxious about him, but when he returned safely to Washington and Lee's Army had gone home and every one seemed so happy in the near approach of Peace that I had thought all danger was past. But now I can see he had got to the place Moses had when God *took him*, he came to the place where *God said* I have caused thee to see it with thine eyes but thou shall not go over to possess it. And now I feel to say, O My Father, President Lincoln is *dead* and send us a Joshua to lead the People and endow him with wisdom and knowledge that he may lead them as faithfully as Joshua of old.

"Oh Mary what fearful, what responsible times we are living in, and it becomes us all to daily pray, Lord what wilt thou have me to do.

"But I must change my theme or I shall fill my sheet with this sad subject and in fact I can hardly think on any thing else. I could tell you how our City is draped in mourning and all business is suspended and the mourners go about the streets, and next Thursday was set apart for our Great Jubilee and now it is to be observed as a day of fasting and prayer. . . .

"Jane says I must tell you that she and Abells wife had a political battle a short time since. She was denouncing the Administration and Old Abe Lincoln in bitter terms and Jane replied to it. She is a perfect Cecesh, or Copperhead as they are called here. And Mary, all such are now rejoicing at the Assassination of our good President."

– Sophia Morton (Williams) Harris,[208] citizen,
Hamburg, N.Y., April 18, 1865

"The army is feeling very sad and gloomy in consequence of President Lincol[n']s death. We feel that we have lost a father and a friend and the country its head. The indignation of the men is great and general. The sadness is general throughout the whole army. Woe to his assassin if he should fall into the hands of our soldiers."

– Assistant Surgeon Edwin R. Brush, 2nd Vermont
Infantry, Burkeville, Va., April 19, 1865

"The young people were at our house one afternoon to practice some music for exhibition. We were singing when we received the sad news that A. Lincoln was dead. Jane Sherman stood by and she said, 'It can't be true, it is too good to be true.' As soon as Emily heard it she went out and told Pa. He was of course feeling very sad, and when he heard what Jane said, he became very indignant and he came in the parlor and asked Jane if she meant what she said. She replied that she did. Pa then told her that any person who would utter such words or harbor such wishes against the President, who had shown himself worthy of the love and honor of every true loyal citizen, such a person was not welcome in his house and the sooner they left the better. But Pa said if she did not mean what she said, he would recall all that he had said. She then said that she only said it to see if I would be angry. Shortly after, Mary O— came in and upon hearing the news said she was glad of it. Jane told her that she had just been lectured for saying the same thing. Mary says—well, let's leave, and they left."

– Nellie Augusta Bernard,[209] citizen,
Charlton, N.Y., April 23, 1865

"What a sad thing, the death of the President. What a damnable act. Just on the eve of peace and such a good man to [the] South, one of the best friends of the soldiers, and to those who he ought to [have] hung instead of pardoning. It cast a sad gloom over the City of Raleigh, and the soldiers were so exasperated that they were going to burn the place, but the people seem to deplore the loss as much as our people, and the papers here speak of Mr. Lincoln very highly, and say he was the 'best friend the whole South ever had.' It will retard peace, but it must come sooner or later."

– Joseph B. Texido, 47th New York Infantry,
Raleigh, N.C., April 25, 1865

"How dose the Peopel of Connecticut take the Sad death of President Lincoln   Evvry thing here is draped in morning   I tell you our country has lost a grate & good man one witch will nevver be forgotton   Andy Johnson is now our President   I think he will make us a good leder   But I tell you one thing he will be rough on the Rebbel leders   He wont Show them So mutch lenity [leniency?] as Abreham did and they know it I think this War is about to an end the time is not far distance when peice will be proclamd through our land."[210]

– Channing S. Clark, Veteran Reserve Corps,
Jeffersonville, Ind., April 25, 1865

"I think one of the most outrageous murders ever committed was that of murdering the President and Secretary Seward. If I could catch a hold of the assassins, I would cut them up in small pieces. Hanging is too good for them. They ought to make a ring and put him in and then put some brush around him and then set it on fire and push it up to him closer and closer and would make him confess all. If he would not do it, I would burn him alive. I am glad President Lincoln lived so long as to see the end of this Great Rebellion, which he has accomplished. I think the rebels have not gained any thing by murdering the President. I think they have killed a friend not an enemy. I always thought Lincoln was a little too lineal [lenient?] to the rebels, but it might have been all for the best. President Johnson, I think, will be a little more severe on the rebels."

– Samuel Musser Fry Jr.,[211] citizen,
Lincoln, Pa., April 25, 1865

"The Surrender of Johnston to Gen'l Grant[212] was unknown to you when you wrote as also the capture and killing of J. Wilkes Booth the assassin and his comrade. They have now all been caught except *Surratt* and he will be caught also ere very long. Booth was a desperate character, as is shown by his stubbornness before he was killed.

"I saw the [late] President at Independence Hall last Sunday, in company with brother Charles. Although there were thousands of *civilians* who could not get in to see our late President, we soldiers could get in without the least trouble, always walking ahead of the whole crowd. I had a fine view of him as I took my time to it, while citizens were hurried through as fast as they could go. Charles was in to see him twice. I went in in the evening after which Charles went

Lincoln's hearse rests outside of the Arch Street Methodist Episcopal Church in Philadelphia. (Lincoln Financial Foundation Collection, courtesy of the Allen County Public Library and the Indiana State Museum and Historic Sites)

out to camp with me as he stayed all night, having a pass for twenty-four hours."

– Anthony Robert Fraser, 186th Pennsylvania Infantry,
Philadelphia, Pa., April 29, 1865

"Yes, Gittie, the assassination of our President proved but too true. You ask, can the northern soldiers ever look upon the South with the least degree of respect? I think if they were again called upon to fight the southern Traitor, *Rebel*, or *assassins*, whatever they may be called (none of those names being appropriate for them), their watchword would be, 'remember our President.' While they know it was a northern man[213] who held the weapon that killed our much lamented President, they also *know* and *bear* in mind that it was *treason* [that] fired it, and that too approved by J. Davis, and more of the leaders of the so-called Confederate States. But Confederate States no more. Yes, Gittie, words will but feebly express our grief for our President at this particular time. Still, I think his successor a very able man and will not show *much* mercy to Rebels. . . . *How sad* is the fate of our much beloved President. I wish the assassins could be caught and their fate left to be decided with the soldiers. They would meet their just doom in a short time, I will warrant you. His death has caused, I think I may safely say, the most general mourning throughout the land of any person ever known, and it seems so much worse at this particular time, when the whole nation were rejoicing over recent victories, and as we thought were about to see the war satisfactorily settled. The *nation* and the people, and *soldiers*, have lost one of their *truest* friends, and I think the most of them appreciate his worth."

– Thomas Richard Petrie, 152nd New York Infantry,
Burkeville Junction, Va., April 29, 1865

"I arrived at Albany [New York] just after the remains of the President had left and learning that they were to stop at Buffalo I took the first train for there as I thought it might be interesting to witness the procession there. We arrived just as his remains were taken from the cars, & witnessed the splendid reception of the group & the showy hearse drawn by 6 white horses handsomely decorated with black & the usual shows of carriages & military bands of marine[s] & a great crowd of people. After viewing the remains in a hall where it was placed on exhibition, I took the cars for the Niagara Falls & Suspension Bridge, where I arrived in due time witnessing that mighty structure, & returning to the falls by first train, visited all the wonders of our side of the River, crossed over to the Island, &c. &c., & ret[urne]d to Buffalo in time to see the [funeral] procession leave for Cleveland & I started 2 hours after arriving at Cleveland in the morning, just after the procession, from there I soon started for Cincinnati."

– Unidentified citizen, Trenton, Ohio, April 30, 1865

"Gertie, for some time back our joys and sorrows have been alternate. One day we are rejoicing over a great victory achieved by some General in the field. The next *we*, with the *whole nation* mourn the untimely *death* of a beloved President. The great statesman, the unyielding patriot, the glorious magistrate is no more. The silent tomb will soon contain all that is earthly of Pres. Lincoln. The *Army weeps*, and a mighty nation mourns, yes friend and *foe*."

– Hamilton McClurg, 102nd Ohio Infantry,
Decatur, Ala., May 1, 1865

"Since the assassination of Lincoln, excitement runs high in this country; in San Francisco resulting in riots and mobs. Several arrests have been made through the state. In Colusa County, just below here, some 6 or 8 of the most prominent men have been arrested for being '*accessories after the fact*' to the assassination of Abraham Lincoln, and some 20 men have taken refuge in the foot-hills to prevent being arrested. Excitement here is dying down now I think."

– John Kingree France,[214] citizen,
Dayton, Calif., May 1, 1865

"What sad news that was of our Beloved Presidents death. They have caught the Assassin but I [am] sorry they could not have taken him alive. I would [have] liked to have been where you were, then I could have seen him and all of those officers. We had quite a sad time in Corry. Almost every house & store were draped in mourning. They preached his funeral sermon. Elder Wilson and Elder Staples & Mr. Merrils and several others were the speakers. They had the sermon in the Baptist Church but there was not room for more than half of the people so they had speaking out doors also. They had their flag at half mast draped and a splendid banner To the memory of Abraham Lincoln on one side & some thing else on the other side which I cannot remember now."

– Unidentified "Alice," citizen, Corry, Pa., May 1, 1865

"By the way I see by the papers that the body of Booth[215] was sunk in the Potomac a few nights ago. By the way I should like to know what David and Horatio thinks or says about the assassination of Lincoln. . . . Well, I guess there is not quite so much chance for those Rebel Leaders to get pardoned with Andrew Johnson for President as there was when Abraham Lincoln was alive, and I hope they will all be caught and hung. That is all the hurt I wish them."

– Capt. Joseph H. Prime,[216] 7th US Colored Infantry,
Point of Rocks, Va., May 2, 1865

John Wilkes Booth. (Lincoln Financial Foundation Collection, courtesy of the Allen County Public Library and the Indiana State Museum and Historic Sites)

This extraordinary, rare image shows the "Assassination Sympathizers" being publicly punished at Chattanooga in April 1865. (Collection of C. Paul Loane)

"We were rather jubilant over the fall of Richmond and Petersburg, the surrender of Lee's Army. It is hardly necessary for me to tell you that the death of our President cast a gloom over every thing with the exception of a few Rebels and butternuts. There were a few Rebs collected together at a house near the camp of Co. I of this Regt. the evening of his death and having quite a jubilee over the sad intelligence, but their rejoicing was of short duration. Co. I went for them as soon as they found out what they were at, thrashed the men and sent them to the Mil. Prison, turned the women out of doors and fired the house. There were a few men who bear the name of Soldier that rejoiced at the death of the President. Such are now working on the most public streets of Chattanooga (or at least all such that [are] near this place) with a ball and chain attached to one foot, or rather ankle, and a card tied on their back with these two words, Assassination Sympathizer printed in large letters on them so that every person that can read or spell may see for what they are working there for. They ought to have their heads shaved and be drummed out of the service."

– George Warren Campbell, Veteran Volunteer Engineering Corps, Chattanooga, Tenn., May 2, 1865

"you ask what I think about our new presedent   I think he is a *greater* man for the times than Mr Lincoln but he never will be loved as he was   *he* had a *great* & *good* heart   they loved him for his goodness—not for his greatness   I do not say that he was not a great man but he was good and that is why he was great (because president) and used his power for goodness and *mercy*   But Jonson will deal with the rebels as well as *any* man we could have and he is as loyal as any man that *lives* and he is a man of the people."

– Unidentified soldier, 105th Pennsylvania Infantry, Fort Reynolds, Va., May 4, 1865

"What an awful thing, the killing of Abe *Lincoln*. Did you ever see or hear of such a time? But they are all Union men in this part of the country. Every body is so sorry when some of them is glad in their hearts if they dared express their sentiments openly. But they are afraid to now."

– Mary Louise Meeker,[217] citizen, Lodi, N.Y., May 6, 1865

"just look at the mourning all over our land and nation brought about by this cursed hell deserving rebellion   ought it not to fall. I would say tear on, tear on [and] finish the work father Abraham undertook to do,   though we have to mourn the loss of a nations preserver we have still confidence in the machinery running enjineered by our most worthy Andrew Johnson that it grind out and meet out justice to each and every one,   they see the hand writing on the wall

"Jeff [Davis] and his accomplices are moving   I see in yesterday['s] paper there is one million dollars is offered for him & his cabinet

Jeff is implicated in the assassin[ation] of Abraham oh that they may receive their just rewards here at least."

– Frederick Newton Barger,[218] citizen,
Concord, Ohio, May 7, 1865

"I did not particularly write you relative to my trip from New York City to Buffalo with the remains of the Late President Lincoln. The cortege arrived in New York on Monday the 24th of April at 10 o'clock in the forenoon. The 7th Regt. N.Y.S. National Guard acted as escort and thousands of people lined the streets. The remains were taken to the City Hall. A guard was placed around it at some distance from it so as to leave an open space—and inside of which and on the steps at south side and about one thousand German singers who chanted a requiem for the dead while the corpse was being conveyed into the building, and places prepared for it at one side of what is called the Governors room. After being placed 'in state' the people were allowed to view the remains. The procession for that purpose was formed on the east side and extended down Chatham Street for nearly a mile. This solemn procession continued from 1 o'clock on the 24th until 11 o'clock on the 25th of April. Twenty-four hours without interruption. On the west side all those having passes were allowed to enter. All night long, with most remarkable patience, the crowds persisted in their endeavors to get a glance at the face of the honored dead. It is said that at least 125,000 viewed the remains and probably as many more were disappointed—people from the country, from New England, and the country adjacent to New York, Brooklyn, Williamsburgh, and Jersey City all getting into line and waiting for hours—many giving up in despair.

"I cannot attempt [to] describe the pageant of the 25th. The newspapers have attempted it but have failed to do full justice. The procession moved at one o'clock from the City Hall up Broadway to 14th St., then west to 5th Avenue, then up the Avenue to 34th Street,

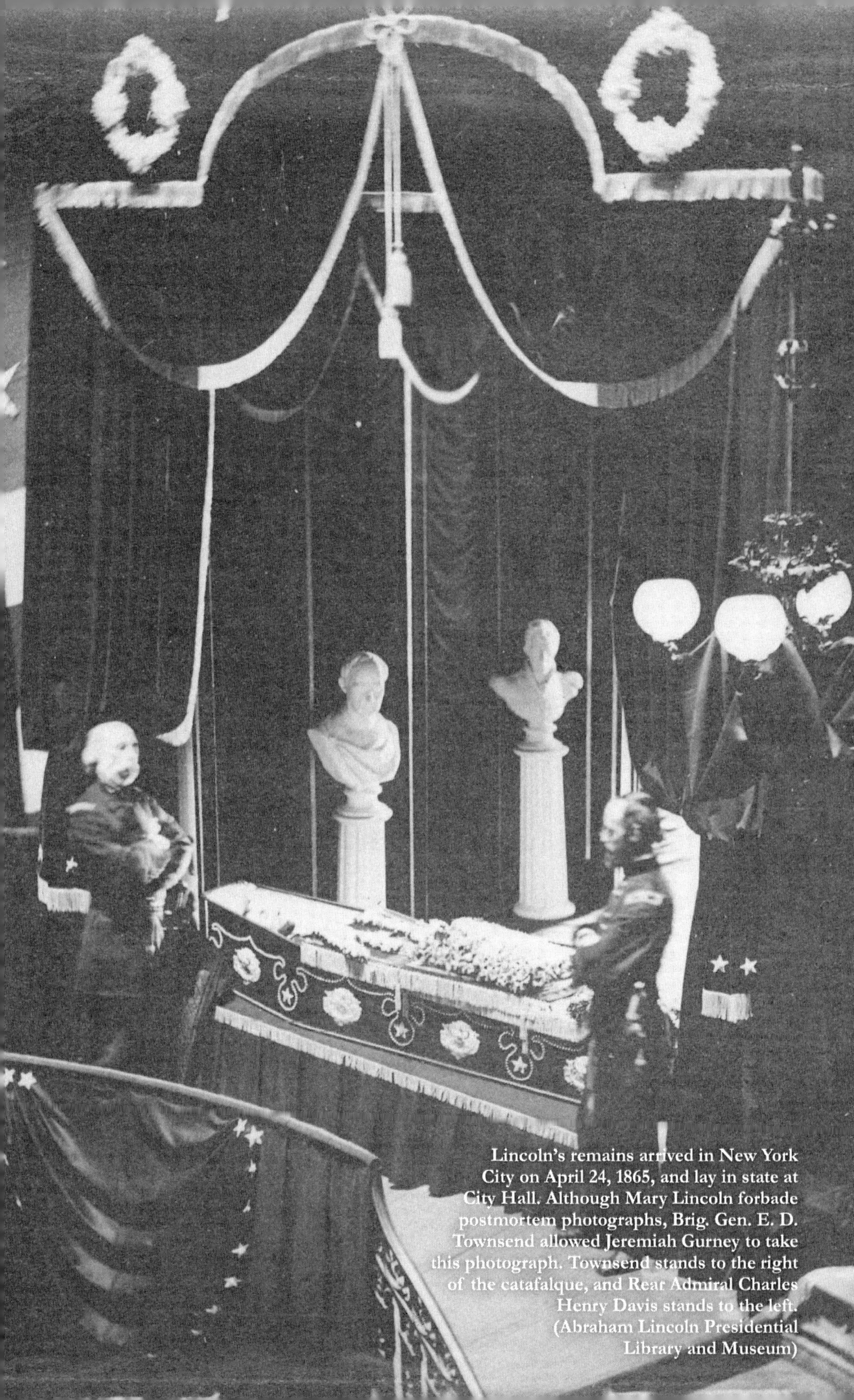

Lincoln's remains arrived in New York City on April 24, 1865, and lay in state at City Hall. Although Mary Lincoln forbade postmortem photographs, Brig. Gen. E. D. Townsend allowed Jeremiah Gurney to take this photograph. Townsend stands to the right of the catafalque, and Rear Admiral Charles Henry Davis stands to the left. (Abraham Lincoln Presidential Library and Museum)

then along 34th St. to 9th Av., thence down 9th Avenue to the Depot [at 30th Street and 11th Avenue]. The catafalque in which the coffin was placed was manufactured for the occasion and cost over $2,000. It was a most splendid affair—& was drawn by sixteen gray horses covered with black broadcloth trimmed with silver fringe—the cloth extending nearly to the ground. Each horse led by a groom. It is said, and I have no doubt with truth, that over one million of people took part in and witnessed this the greatest funeral procession of which we have any account in the world. It was immense. Thirty eight carriages only were allowed in the procession (and only one private carriage, that of the venerable Lieut. Gen. Winfield Scott) which contained the state & city authorities and representatives of the several states who accompanied the remains from Washington and the Guard of Honor. . . .

"We took the train for Albany at ½ 4 o'clock P.M. The cars were beautifully ornamented and draped in mourning. Arrived in Albany at ten o'clk P.M. I cannot give you all the incidents along the route, but it seemed like a panorama of people gathered along the road and at the several villages—paying by their reverential and solemn behavior their tribute of respect—to the departed Emancipator.

"At Albany the Military received and escorted the remains to the Assembly Chamber which had been prepared for its reception. At about 4 A.M. the people were allowed to enter, and thus could avail themselves of this opportunity to behold him for whom the nation was in mourning. At one o'clock on the 26th the procession in Albany was formed and after passing through the principal streets escorted the remains to the cars which moved off for Buffalo at 4 o'clock P.M. Arriving at St. Johnsbury [Vermont], we stopped for ten [minutes], the station here being splendidly draped for the occasion. Herkimer & Utica, Rome, Syracuse, Rochester, and in fact all along the route to Buffalo, were awaiting the train. The militia organizations, common councils, [and] choirs were out waiting for the funeral train to pass, all seeming anxious to get but a sight of the

This image depicts Lincoln's funeral procession as it passed along Broadway. The funeral car, which was pulled by a team of 16 horses, is in the foreground. Thousands of spectators watched from windows and rooftops. (Library of Congress)

car in which was the mortal remains of him in whom they had placed so much confidence and trust. We arrived in Buffalo at six o'clock in the morning, and after partaking of a breakfast prepared for us, the remains were escorted by the military and citizens to St. James Hall where splendid arrangements had been perfected for the occasion, and as the body was being brou[ght] into the building a choir of 100 voices (St. Cecil Society) chanted a funeral dirge—the most solemn and effective singing I ever heard. The arrangement for viewing the corpse was much better here than in New York or Albany. All who desired had an opportunity. . . .

"After bidding adieu to the Guard of Honor, General [John A.] Dix and the escort, we (the Governor's staff) took the train for Albany again where we arrived at 9 o'ck on the morning of the 28th. Perhaps you will think this a long and tedious account—but excuse me for feeling proud of the position temporarily occupied and regarding the occasion as great historical event, was glad to be so prominently connected with it."

– Edwin Atkins Merritt, Quartermaster General of New York, Albany, N.Y., May 15, 1865

"I *wished* that I could be present at Springfield at the time of the funeral ceremonies. That I never saw Mr. Lincoln when living seems to me *now* a real misfortune. I remember when he spoke in Hillsboro [Illinois] in 1858. I call to mind distinctly my occupation on that day and how, being so very busy, I could not spare the time to visit Hillsboro. . . . I cant remember that I had any knowledge of Mr. Lincoln previous to the time of the meeting of the convention in June 1858, that named him as the opponent of Douglas in the senatorial campaign. Since then my regard for him has grown into almost a passion, and the news of his murder came home to me with all the crushing force of an appalling personal calamity. From the time of that remarkable speech in Springfield in 1858 [the House Divided Address], I never for one moment doubted his honesty, ability, or the correctness of his principles and measures; and though the advanced state of public opinion has called for modifications of the measures of his administration, yet I am not convinced that the measures he adopted at the time were not the best *for* the time. How many of our heroes of this war have lost all the attributes of heroism. The Fremonts, the Sigels, the Butlers etc. Perhaps Butler ought to be expected. He succeeded as an Executive officer but failed deplorably as a military man. But Mr. Lincoln, entering Washington almost as a fugitive 4 years ago, won the admiration of the world by the conduct of affairs of State in the midst of difficulties almost unparalleled, and *dying*, is mourned, not only by his countrymen, but by all peoples."

– Surgeon Humphrey Hughes Hood, 3rd US Colored Heavy Artillery, Memphis, Tenn., May 15, 1865[219]

"I have been down to the city and visit[ed] the Smith Sonians Institute and the Patent office and the Botanic[al] Gardens   I would not [have]

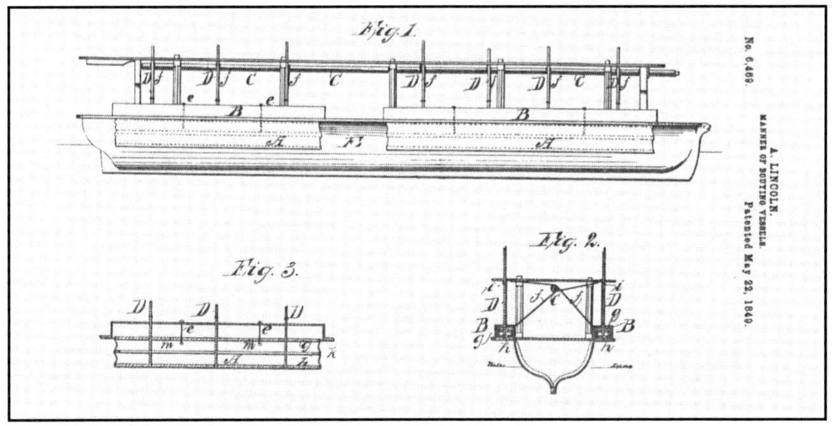

To this day, Lincoln remains the only president to hold a US patent. In 1849 he designed a device for "buoying vessels over shoals." As a young man working on rivers, he had experienced problems when his vessels came aground. (National Archives)

missed it for one hundred Dollar[s]. . . . in the Patent of[fice] you can see the progress of the American people you will find the old Wooden mole Board plow up to the present improvement the greates thing their is a model of a steam boat that Abe Lincoln made it will be preserved as Long as the American people Live."

– William Thomas Applegate,[220] citizen,
Washington, D.C., May 18, 1865

"I will send you a picture of Lincoln in this letter. It is a first rate picture of him. It looks exactly [like] him. Send that picture along. I want to see it."

– George A. Spencer, 7th Rhode Island Infantry,
Alexandria, Va., May 20, 1865

"By reading your letter I discover that I had forgotten a part of it. I discover that you are quite a politician. You state that the copperheads are afraid that Johnson will be harder on them than Lincoln would have been. I hope they are not mistaken. I hope they will be held to the line and strictly brought to an account for their treason and evry traitor either hung or banished from the land, I mean the Leaders of the rebellion. The Leaders of the conspiracy to murder the President and the Leaders of the Knights of the Golden Circle or Sons of Liberty."

– Chaplain Clark C. Phillips, 23rd and 29th Iowa Infantries, ca. May 1865

"*I* am truly thankful that this '*Cruel* War is so nearly at an end.' It seemed as news came over the wire that Lee had surrendered that our whole land was filled with rejoicing. Boston was all excitement. All places of business were closed and all the Military & Fire Companies of Boston and the adjacent towns marched through the principal streets and bells were rung and cannon fired. The 10th of April was a day long to be remembered in Boston. But it seemed that their rejoicing was soon to be turned to mourning. The morning of the 15th *I* shall never forget. As I went to the store every body looked so sad that I wondered what could be the reason of it. Upon entering the [store] I asked one of the salesmen why it was everyone looked so sad. And they said, did you not know that our President had been killed. I could hardly believe it. But upon opening the paper, I found that it must be so. And upon returning home that afternoon the buildings were everywhere draped in mourning. Such a sad sight as Boston presented that week will be long remembered. It seems dreadful that such a good man as Lincoln was should die by the hand of the assassin. I saw J. Wilkes Booth a year ago this month in the Museum. That was the only time I ever went to the Museum. It was his benefit evening. It was a tragical performance. It hardly seems possible he could ever have committed such a crime as he personated that evening."

– Emma E. Davis,[221] citizen, Boston, Mass., May 28, 1865

1866

"We visited [the] Lincoln Tomb at Oak Ridge Cemetery about two miles from this city. I was surprised to see so simple and plain a structure over the remains of so *Great* and *Good* a man. It is a plain brick vault occupying a knoll near the entrance of the Cemetery. It has only the name 'Lincoln' on a marble slab in the front. We sat on that knoll for more than an hour under the shade of several little oaks thinking of the 'Great departed.' I could not help but wish that he could have lived to occupy that seat which is now being disgraced by Andrew Johnson. I plucked some wild flowers growing near his grave and inclose them to you. The Cemetery is a beautiful one and has some splendid monuments in it. Springfield is a very neat little city of some 10 or 12 thousand inhabitants. The streets are wide and regular and has some splendid residences and does a good inland trade."

– George W. Fraser,[222] veteran,
Springfield, Ill., May 26, 1866

Lincoln's remains were held in this vault from December 1865 until 1871, when they were moved to his final resting place up the hill from this location. This 1868 image depicts Ulysses S. Grant visiting the tomb at Oak Ridge Cemetery. (Library of Congress)

1912

"I was at the battle of Fort Stevens [on July 12, 1864] where we lost 280 men in a very short time, and most of the battle was witnessed by the President standing on the parapet of the fort. . . .[223] This all happened in sight and sound of where I happened to be in the line, as the 3rd Vt was the first regiment to the left of the fort and Co. A,

Fort Stevens, on the outskirts of Washington, D.C., as it appeared in 1864. (Library of Congress)

to which I belonged, was on the right, so I was not more than 6 or 8 rods [roughly 100–130 feet] away, so could see the men standing on the fort. But as Mr. Lincoln was surrounded by the others in my direction I could not see him very well, only his hat. I wanted very much to go to the entrance of the fort to see him when he came out, but we were liable to be ordered forward at any moment, so felt obliged to stay in my place. . . . Napoleon the Great has the largest number of words devoted to him of any man in history, but he never had such a place in the hearts of the people as President Lincoln."

– George E. Farrington,[224] veteran,
Elgin, Ill., April 22, 1912

1927

"My Band was orderd to City Point to serenade Abram Lincoln for 3 nights. I Played the best music I had for A Lincoln after Playing ½ hour Mr Lincoln came and putting his hand on my should[er] said Mr. Leader will you please play Dixie, we had not Played [it] for 6 month[s] the Rebs took it for their grand march so we let them have it when the President asked [us] to Play it I said Mr President thats a Confederate tune he replied *It was* but we have captured it now Play Dixie and that made Dixie a National tune by order of President Lincoln & weeve been plaeing it ever since he called for dixie on all three nights."

– William Critchley,[225] veteran, 13th New Hampshire Infantry, Lake Pleasant, Mass., August 31, 1927

Endnotes

1 Michael Robert Buttz (1839–1875) of Liberty, Adams County, Ill., wrote this letter to his cousin.

2 Sen. Stephen A. Douglas (1813–1861), known as "the Little Giant," was Lincoln's Democratic opponent in the Illinois race for US Senate in 1858. He would be the northern Democratic candidate for president in 1860.

3 Sen. Lyman Trumbull (1813–1896) was a Democrat-turned-Republican who had defeated Lincoln in a US Senate race in 1855.

4 The Lecompton Constitution was a proposed pro-slavery state constitution in Kansas. President James Buchanan supported its adoption, but Douglas opposed it. It was overwhelmingly rejected by the voters of Kansas in 1858.

5 This letter appears on stationery featuring a portrait of Lincoln and an image of a flatboat on a river.

6 Most candidates for president in the 19th century "stood" for election (as opposed to "running" for office); Douglas, by contrast, actively campaigned around the country.

7 John Wilson (1790–1877), a native of Augusta County, Va., settled in California in 1849 to work as an Indian agent, then as a navy agent. A former Whig, he supported the Constitutional Union ticket in 1860. This letter was written to an old friend, James William Denver (1817–1892), a Democrat who supported Douglas in 1860.

8 Hannibal Hamlin (1809–1891) of Maine was Lincoln's running mate in the 1860 presidential election.

9 This excerpt from a handwritten speech in favor of the southern Democrat John C. Breckinridge was most likely delivered by George Washington Wortham (1823–1883) at a mass meeting and barbecue held at Buchanan, Granville County, N.C., on October 10, 1860. Wortham rose to the rank of colonel of the 50th North Carolina Infantry during the war.

10 Young men organized into Wide Awake organizations throughout the North to campaign for Lincoln, often holding torchlight processions down city streets at night.

11 Albert Freeman Dow (1844–1922) would go on to serve as an officer in the 4th Massachusetts Infantry. This letter was written to his brother, Wesley (1841–1863).

12 Abolitionist Owen Lovejoy (1811–1864) was a Republican congressman from Illinois.

13 Samuel Galloway (1811–1872), a Republican from Ohio, had served in the US House of Representatives from 1855 to 1857.

14 The 1860 Republican National Convention took place in a Chicago building known as the Wigwam.

15 Frank Gould (1841–1920), a native of Peacham, Vt., moved west in October 1860.

16 During the antebellum period many southern states passed legislation that silenced abolitionist speech. Violence was also used to silence abolitionists in both the North and the South.

17 Vice President John C. Breckinridge (1821–1875), a slaveholder from Kentucky, was the southern Democratic candidate for president in 1860. He served in the US Senate from March 4 to December 4, 1861, before joining the Confederacy as a general and secretary of war.

18 John Bell (1796–1869) of Tennessee ran for president on the Constitutional Union ticket in 1860. His running mate was Edward Everett of Massachusetts.

19 It would have been dangerous for Abbott to vote for Lincoln in the South since voting was a public act in the mid-19th century and everyone at the polls would have known that he had voted for Lincoln. Moreover, in the 19th century the parties printed their own ballots, and there would have been no Republican Party organization to print ballots in most of the South.

20 Joseph Brown Abbott (1835–1892) of Surry, N.H., taught school in Newbern, N.C., for four years before the Civil War.

21 William Elmer Potter (1840–1896) received his law degree from Harvard in 1861 and entered Princeton as a junior in August 1861 (he was part of the class of 1863). In 1862 he enlisted in the 12th New Jersey Infantry, rising to the rank of brevet major in 1866. His diary is held by the Seeley G. Mudd Manuscript Library, Princeton University.

22 South Carolina would not secede until December 20, 1860. These other states followed in January 1861.

23 Following the war, Early appears to have accepted the reality of Confederate defeat. In 1865, he wrote, "The sentiment of the people throughout this region is one of entire submission to the result of the contest. Slavery is universally regarded as extinct, and there is a general and absolute acquiescence in its fate. . . . There is no spirit of further resistance . . . disunionists are now perfectly satisfied with the experiment made." *Wheeling Intelligencer*, September 21, 1865.

24 William T. Early (1817–1874), the owner of 36 slaves in 1860, sent this letter to Septimus Douglass Cabaniss (1815–1889), a lawyer in Huntsville, Ala. (and an alumnus of the University of Virginia), who served in the Alabama state legislature during the Civil War.

25 Ridgely was the eighteen-year-old daughter of a prominent Springfield banker and Democrat. Thanks to Michelle Miller and Christian McWhirter for bringing her diaries to our attention at the Abraham Lincoln Presidential Library and Museum in Springfield, Ill.

26 Andrew G. Curtin (1815–1894), a Republican, served as governor of Pennsylvania from 1861 to 1867.

27 Frederick W. Lauer (1840–1917) of Pottsville, Schuylkill County, Pa., was the son of German immigrants. He later attended Lewisburg University (now Bucknell) and worked in the brewery business.

28 The abolitionist John Brown (1800–1859) raided Harpers Ferry, Va. (now West Virginia), in October 1859 in an attempt to start a widescale slave insurrection in the South. Brown was captured by US Marines under the command of Robert E. Lee and was executed in December for treason against Virginia and murder. His raid led many fearful white southerners to join militia units to be prepared to counteract future slave insurrections.

29 Peter J. Miller (1841–1910), a laborer from Stark County, Ohio, wrote this letter to his uncle George Miller (1804–1867).

30 Little is known about Lizzie Fisher, who sent this letter to her sister Nan.

31 President James Buchanan (1791–1868) was a pro-slavery northern Democrat who believed that secession was unconstitutional but that he had no power to stop it.

32 Judge William Brown (1797–1866) sent this letter to the Rep. John Carey (1792–1875), a Republican from Ohio who served in Congress from 1859 to 1861.

33 While northern Democrats like Stephen A. Douglas advocated for the territories to be able to determine for themselves whether they would permit slavery (this was called "popular sovereignty"), white southerners wanted a federal slave code for the territories. Republicans like Lincoln feared that southerners would win a Supreme Court case that would permit them to take their enslaved property anywhere in the country, including the free states of the North.

34 William H. Seward (1801–1872) served as a US senator from New York from 1849 to 1861, and as secretary of state from 1861 to 1869.

35 In 1858 Seward delivered a speech in which he stated that the North and South were engaged in "an irrepressible conflict between opposing and enduring forces, and it means that the United States must and will, sooner or later, become entirely either a slave-holding nation, or entirely a free-labor nation."

36 Robert McKee Gaston (1840–1863) was a schoolteacher in Mount Pleasant who enlisted with the 100th Pennsylvania Infantry in August 1861. In 1862 he was commissioned a 1st lieutenant in the 1st South Carolina Volunteers (33rd USCT) at Beaufort. He was accidentally killed by a black soldier under his command during a scouting expedition on May 27, 1863. This letter was written to his boyhood friend, Oscar L. Jackson.

37 The Lincoln home at Eighth and Jackson Streets in Springfield, Ill., is the only home the president ever owned.

38 Ridgely was nineteen when she met Lincoln at the public reception at his home on February 6, 1861. Although she was a Democrat who opposed Lincoln's election (see her November 11, 1860, letter), she appears to have had a change of heart about him.

39 Henry P. Hubbell (1827-1892), a Democrat, went on to serve as lieutenant colonel of the 3rd New York Infantry. His papers are held at Princeton University.

40 In a short speech delivered at Indianapolis on February 11, 1861, Lincoln spoke obliquely about the right of the federal government to hold its forts, to collect duties on imports, and to deliver the mail, asking, "Would any or all of these things be coercion? Do the lovers of the Union contend that they will resist coercion or invasion of any State, understanding that any or all of these would be coercing or invading a State?"

41 Nathan Howard Jr. (1808–1876), a New York City attorney, wrote this letter to his brother, Jerome Bonaparte Howard (1819–1864), who was living in the Midwest. Jerome enlisted in the 123rd Ohio Infantry and later died of disease as a prisoner of war at Andersonville. This letter is courtesy of Justin Hawkins.

42 Hoping to capitalize on the crowd coming into New York City to see the president-elect, P. T. Barnum announced in advance that his museum would be exhibiting "The Great Lincoln Turkey"—alleged to be a 40-pounder—that would be presented to Lincoln on Inauguration Day. New Yorkers were invited to come to the museum not only to see the turkey but also to "use its windows and balconies to observe Lincoln's departure from the city."

43 The author of this letter, John Booton ("Boot") Hill (1841–1913), was living in New York City before the war, apparently working as a clerk for his uncle, Major Henry Hill (1816–1866), who was the army paymaster of New York at the time. Henry's resignation from the US army was announced in June 1861 when he decided to cast his lot with the Confederacy. Shortly after Virginia seceded from the Union, Boot enlisted on April 23, 1861, at Madison Court House to serve in the 7th Virginia Infantry. He was later detailed to P. G. T. Beauregard's headquarters at Manassas and in the Pay Department of the State of Virginia, eventually mustering out as a major. This letter is in the Hill Family Papers, Virginia Museum of History and Culture, Richmond, Va.

44 Andrew Horatio Reeder (1807–1864) was governor of the Territory of Kansas from 1854 to 1855.

45 Samuel W. Pennypacker (1843–1916) would go on to serve as governor of Pennsylvania from 1903 to 1907. This letter from Pennypacker to his uncle, February 23, 1861, is held at the Historical Society of Pennsylvania.

46 Detective Allan Pinkerton (1819–1884) learned of credible assassination threats in Baltimore and persuaded Lincoln to travel through the city in disguise the night before originally scheduled.

47 A native of Philadelphia who had settled in Savannah during the antebellum era, Charles A. Greiner (1810–1865) was arrested for treason while traveling in Philadelphia in May 1861 for his role as a militiaman in capturing Fort Pulaski. After spending some time in jail, he was released from custody because there were no federal courts operating in Georgia.

48 William Winston Seaton (1785–1866) published the Washington *National Intelligencer* from 1812 to 1860 with his brother-in-law, Joseph Gales. Seaton also had served as mayor of Washington from 1840 to 1850.

49 Montgomery Blair (1813–1883), a conservative Republican, served as Lincoln's postmaster general from 1861 to 1864.

50 Blair lived in a home called Falklands near his father, Francis P. Blair, who lived at Silver Spring, Md., on the outskirts of Washington, DC. Falklands was burned by Confederate general Jubal A. Early's men in July 1864 during the raid on Washington.

51 Speaker of the House Schuyler Colfax (1823–1885) of South Bend, Ind., served in the US House of Representatives from 1855 to 1869 (including as Speaker of the House from 1863 to 1869), before serving as Ulysses S. Grant's vice president from 1869 to 1873.

52 Levi Clark (1799–1862) of Newark, N.J., sent this letter to his brother-in-law, Charles M. Heaton of South Bend, Ind.

53 James Webster Carr (1824–1875) rose to the rank of lieutenant colonel of the 2nd New Hampshire Infantry.

54 Robert Elliott (1826–1884) was an English immigrant who came to the United States in the 1850s.

55 Andrew Johnson (1808–1875) of Tennessee was the only southerner to maintain his seat in the US Senate. During the war he served as military governor of Tennessee, and in the 1864 presidential election he was Lincoln's running mate.

56 Democrats like Stephen A. Douglas frequently race-baited, claiming that Republicans wanted to "amalgamate" the white and black races.

57 In the years before the Civil War, northern states enacted personal liberty laws, which made it more difficult for southern slaveholders to recapture fugitive slaves who had escaped into the North. In 1842, the US Supreme Court declared such laws unconstitutional.

58 Benjamin Wade (1800–1878), a Republican from Ohio, served in the US Senate from 1851 to 1869.

59 An abolitionist and perennial aspirant for the presidency, Salmon P. Chase (1808–1873) served as governor of Ohio (1856–1860), a US senator (1849–1855 and 1861), Lincoln's first secretary of the treasury (1861–1864), and chief justice of the US Supreme Court (1864–1873).

60 *New-York Tribune* editor Horace Greeley (1811–1872) was a perennial thorn in Lincoln's side during the Civil War. In 1862, Lincoln publicly called Greeley "an old friend, whose heart I have always supposed to be right," but in private, Lincoln likened him to an "old shoe—good for nothing now, whatever he has been."

61 Eleven-year-old Wyly J. Smith of Eastern Tennessee wrote this letter from Missouri, where he was likely staying with relatives. The recipient, James Knox Polk Saylor (1839–1919), was a schoolteacher where Smith was raised and likely had been Smith's teacher. Smith's father, Peter Smith (1828–1902), joined the 1st Tennessee (Union) Cavalry.

62 Daniel D. Westervelt (ca. 1828–1896) inherited a New York ship-building business from his father, former New York City mayor Jacob Aaron Westervelt (1800–1879). This letter was written to his "dear cousin" Mary Anna Manning in Missouri.

63 This letter is signed "Samuel Tromore, Captain of the Palmetto guards," but that was almost certainly a pseudonym used by Edward N. Fuller (1824–1904) to protect his identity. This letter is courtesy of Richard Weiner.

64 The United States and England each maintained its own Africa Squadron to patrol for slavers on the Atlantic Ocean; however, Lincoln recalled US warships in 1861 for use in the Civil War.

65 In 1832, President Andrew Jackson threatened to send 50,000 troops to South Carolina when that state nullified the federal tariff and contemplated secession from the Union. Sen. Henry Clay of Kentucky helped usher a "compromise" tariff through Congress that lowered rates, but Sen. John C. Calhoun of South Carolina continued to talk of secession until his death in 1850.

66 Likely written by Henry W. Morgan (1840–1885), an immigrant from Wales who would later enlist in the 15th Pennsylvania Cavalry.

67 In March and April 1861, Secretary of State Seward suggested that Lincoln abandon Fort Sumter to appease the South. Privately, Seward had also encouraged the US to go to war with a foreign nation in order to unify the North and South.

68 Gideon Welles (1802–1878), a newspaperman from Connecticut, served as secretary of the navy from 1861 to 1869.

69 Caleb Blood Smith (1808–1864) of Indiana served as Lincoln's first secretary of the interior.

70 Union forces would abandon Gosport Navy Yard at Norfolk, Va., on April 21, 1861, setting it on fire before they departed and destroying several important warships to prevent them from falling into Confederate hands. Afterward the Confederates salvaged the USS *Merrimack*, converting her into the CSS *Virginia*, an ironclad warship that would battle the USS *Monitor* on March 9, 1862.

71 Dr. Clement B. Hayden (1811–1885), a native of Maine, moved to Maysville, Ark. He sent this letter to his nephew, William P. Hayden, who was back in Maine.

72 Winfield Scott (1786–1866), a native of Virginia, was the commanding general of the Union army at the beginning of the Civil War.

73 Katherine St. Clair Greenleaf (1856–1923), daughter of the writer Katherine "Kate" Pinckard (1835–1905).

74 Lydia (Judd) Stockwell (1828–1919) of Massachusetts moved to Iowa in 1857.

75 Brig. Gen. Joseph K. Mansfield (1803–1862) commanded the Department of Washington in the spring and summer of 1861. He was mortally wounded at Antietam in September 1862.

76 During the second Lincoln-Douglas debate at Freeport, Ill., on August 27, 1858, Stephen A. Douglas articulated what became known as the Freeport Doctrine: that while territorial legislatures could not outright prohibit slavery, they could "effectively prevent the introduction of it into their midst" by electing antislavery representatives who would enact "unfriendly legislation."

77 During his one term in Congress (1847–1849), Lincoln vehemently opposed the Mexican War. Using words that would later come back to haunt him, he declared, "Any people anywhere, being inclined and having the power, have the *right* to rise up, and shake off the existing government, and for a new one that suits them better. This is a most valuable,—a most sacred right—a right, which we hope and believe, is to liberate the world. Nor is this right confined to cases in which the whole people of an existing government, may choose to exercise it. Any portion of such people that *can*, *may* revolutionize, and make their *own*, of so much of the territory as they inhabit."

78 This letter was sent to Mrs. Eunice S. Kingsley of Clinton, Maine.

79 Jefferson Davis (1808–1889) of Mississippi was president of the Confederate States of America.

80 Horace Moore Polk (1819–1883) was a planter on Bayou Bartholomew in Morehouse Parish, La. A former state legislator in both Tennessee and Louisiana, he supported Stephen A. Douglas in the Democratic conventions at Charleston and Baltimore in 1860. Although he initially opposed secession, he followed Louisiana into the Confederacy.

81 Following the Union defeat at Bull Run on July 21, 1861, Lincoln called Maj. Gen. George B. McClellan (1826–1885) to take command of what would become known as the Army of the Potomac.

82 Joy mistakenly refers to Smith's division as a brigade.

83 Simon Cameron (1799–1889) of Pennsylvania, one of the most corrupt politicians of the 19th century, served as Lincoln's first secretary of war.

84 Cameron had been on the board of directors of the Northern Central Railroad since its founding in 1854 and by the time of the Civil War owned a large share of the company's stock. During the war, the Northern Central carried Union soldiers from central Pennsylvania south to Baltimore.

85 Maj. Gen. John C. Fremont (1813–1890) had been the first Republican candidate for president in 1856. As the Union military commander in Missouri, he issued an order freeing the slaves of disloyal masters on August 30, 1861; however, Lincoln revoked the order since Missouri was a loyal state with its constitutional rights intact. Lincoln later removed Fremont from command on November 2, 1861.

86 In October 1861, Sen. John C. Breckinridge published an address "to the people of Kentucky" on the pages of the Louisville *Courier* in which he argued that Lincoln, Republicans in Congress and the state legislature, and "northern invaders" had violated state rights and individual rights. "I intend to resist," he intoned. "To this course we are impelled by our highest sense of duty and the irresistible instincts of manhood."

87 In Homer's *Iliad*, the Myrmidons (sometimes Myrmidones) were the Achaeans' best troops and were commanded by the Trojan War hero Achilles. They were sometimes seen as worker-ants who carried out orders unquestioningly.

88 Charles Slaughter Morehead (1802–1868) had served as governor of Kentucky from 1855 to 1859. An outspoken critic of the Lincoln administration, he was imprisoned for disloyalty from September 1861 until January 1862.

89 November 20, 1861, at Munson's Hill, Bailey's Crossroads.

90 Prince de Joinville (1818–1900) of France served on General McClellan's staff during the first year of the war.

91 This word may be "thundering."

92 Henry Augustus Sims (1832–1875), a native of Philadelphia, moved to Canada in 1851 to work as a civil engineer for a railroad. By 1858 he had become a naturalized Canadian citizen, although he returned to the United States in 1866.

93 As Kentuckians, several of Mary Lincoln's brothers and in-laws joined the Confederacy.

94 Maj. John Watt had served as White House gardener since Franklin Pierce's presidency.

95 During the summer of 1861, a select congressional committee led by Republican John Fox Potter of Wisconsin investigated the loyalty of federal employees. Although Potter's committee preferred charges against Watt, Lincoln chose not to act upon them. Michael Burlingame has cataloged Watt's corrupt behavior in *Abraham Lincoln: A Life* (2008), chap. 25.

96 Ira Cole (1792–1871), a veteran of the War of 1812, wrote this letter to his son-in-law, Asa Lyman Hazelton (1807–1906), who was chief clerk in the Treasury Department.

97 This private note to Lord John Russell is held at the British National Archives in Kew.

98 Adolphus Clark (1805–1885), a native of New York, settled in Illinois in 1836.

99 George Quint (1803–1877) sent this letter to his son, Rev. Alonzo Hall Quint (1828–1896), chaplain of the 2nd Massachusetts Infantry.

100 Charles M. Heaton (1805–1899) settled in South Bend, Ind., in 1833, where he became a civic leader. As a Whig-turned-Republican, he was close with South Bend editor, journalist, and politician Schuyler Colfax, who rewarded him with a position in the federal land office in Washington in 1860, where he remained for the next 20 years.

101 For the first half of the war, Lincoln supported the voluntary colonizing of freed slaves to other parts of the world, including in Africa, the Caribbean, and Latin America.

102 Ann Crane Heaton, a milliner, married Charles M. Heaton in 1833.

103 Lincoln decided to issue an emancipation proclamation during the summer of 1862 but delayed issuing the document until after a Union battlefield victory. On September 22, 1862, five days after the Battle of Antietam, he issued a preliminary emancipation proclamation, which stated that he would issue a final proclamation on January 1, 1863, if the Confederate states did not return to the Union.

104 This word is difficult to decipher. It may be "adopted" or "attempted" or something entirely different.

105 The Battle of Antietam on September 17, 1862, was the bloodiest day in American history. Although it was a tactical draw, Lincoln considered it a victory because Robert E. Lee had crossed the Potomac River into Maryland, and then recrossed back into Virginia following the battle. Five days later Lincoln issued his preliminary emancipation proclamation.

106 Rhode Island politician Ambrose Burnside (1824–1881) suffered disastrous defeats at Fredericksburg (December 13, 1862) and Petersburg (July 30, 1864).

107 The 44th New York Infantry, known as Ellsworth's Avengers, was named after Lincoln's young friend Elmer Ellsworth, who had been killed on May 24, 1861, when he took down a Confederate flag in Alexandria, Va. Ellsworth had been colonel of the 11th New York Fire Zouaves.

108 After Lincoln removed McClellan from command on November 7, 1862, the general wrote a farewell message in which he conveyed his "love and gratitude" to the troops. He concluded, "We shall ever be comrades in supporting the Constitution of our country and the nationality of its people."

109 The state of Iowa passed legislation permitting soldiers to vote on September 17, 1862, well before most other northern states enacted such legislation. (This is discussed in greater detail in the 1864 chapter.)

110 Clement L. Vallandigham (1820–1871) of Ohio was an outspoken Peace Democrat and critic of Lincoln and the war. He was arrested for disloyal speech in May 1863. Following his conviction by a military commission, Lincoln had him banished to the Confederacy.

111 The fifth article of war, which was published in the *Revised United States Army Regulations of 1861*, prohibited soldiers from using "contemptuous or disrespectful words" against the president, vice president, Congress, or governor and legislature of any state in which the troops were quartered.

112 Lincoln issued the final Emancipation Proclamation on January 1, 1863.

113 Governor Andrew G. Curtin did not move to withdraw Pennsylvania troops from federal service.

114 David Tod (1805–1868), a Democrat-turned-Republican, served as governor of Ohio from 1862 to 1864.

115 Edwin M. Stanton (1814–1869) replaced Simon Cameron as secretary of war in January 1862, serving in that position until 1868.

116 Henry Wager Halleck (1815–1872), known as "Old Brains," served as general in chief of the US armies from 1862 to 1864. Because Halleck was a good organizer, Lincoln hoped that he would help devise Union strategy. However, Halleck disappointed Lincoln, who allegedly stated that he was "little more than a first rate clerk."

117 Samuel Newell Holmes (1823–1900), a nephew of Oliver Wendell Holmes Sr., wrote this letter to his wife, Mary Elizabeth (Beach) Holmes (1823–1881), and their six children during a visit to the nation's capital. Holmes datelined his letter, "Presidents House," meaning that he likely wrote it in the White House.

118 Congress enacted a conscription law on March 3, 1863. Under the initial law, men ages 20 to 45 were liable to be drafted.

119 Sarah Eliza "Lizzie" (Wilson) Rice (1842–1928) sent this letter to her husband John Birchard Rice (1832–1893), an army surgeon with the 10th and 22nd Ohio Infantries.

120 Sarah Ann Adams (1808–1897) wrote this to her only son, Charles H. Adams (1844–1930) of the 15th New Hampshire Infantry, a nine-month regiment.

121 Willis F. Riddick (1811–1871) wrote this to Adeline Burr Currier (born 1845) of Warren County, N.C., who became his third wife in October 1866. He was employed in the Confederate postal service in Richmond during the war.

122 Daniel S. Dickinson (1800–1866), a War Democrat, served as attorney general of New York from 1862 to 1863. During the presidential election of 1864 he supported Lincoln's reelection.

123 Maj. Gen. Benjamin F. Butler (1818–1893), an antebellum Democrat who had voted for Jefferson Davis to be the Democratic nominee for president in 1860, became a Radical Republican during the war.

124 Former President Martin Van Buren (1782–1862) was a War Democrat who supported the Union.

125 Samuel Medary (1801–1864), a Peace Democrat in Columbus, Ohio, edited the antiwar newspaper *The Crisis.*

126 New York City Mayor Fernando Wood (1812–1881) and his brother, Congressman Benjamin Wood (1820–1900), were notorious Peace Democrats who were suspected of favoring southern secession. During the war, Benjamin edited the anti-Lincoln New York *Daily News.*

127 Maj. Gen. Joseph Hooker (1814–1879) took command of the Army of the Potomac after Ambrose Burnside's humiliating defeat at Fredericksburg and the subsequent disastrous "Mud March" in January 1863. While Hooker exhibited great bombast, he lost his nerve at the Battle of Chancellorsville in May 1863, allowing the Confederates to win a decisive victory with far fewer numbers.

128 Maj. Gen. John Sedgwick (1813–1864) commanded the Army of the Potomac's Sixth Corps.

129 This was actually Col. John Lee of the 55th Ohio Infantry.

130 According to the diary of Attorney General Edward Bates, April 4, 1863, Lincoln's son Tad (1853–1871) accompanied the president and Mary Lincoln on the trip. The Washington *Evening Star* of April 10, 1863, reported that the other boy was Gustave Albert Schuman, Tad's "companion . . . not yet fourteen years old, and who was with General Kearney through all his battles except the last one." The *Evening Star* reported that both boys were "mounted on fine horses and attracted considerable attention."

131 In April and May 1863, Adjutant General Lorenzo Thomas (1804–1875) addressed white Union soldiers in the Western Theater regarding Lincoln's new policy of enlisting black soldiers. At Helena, Arkansas, he declared, "The policy of the Administration must be carried out, and no opposition on the part of officers and soldiers will be allowed."

132 Confederate General Thomas Jonathan "Stonewall" Jackson (1824–1863) was mortally wounded by friendly fire at the Battle of Chancellorsville on May 2, 1863. He died on May 10.

133 During the Civil War the Confederate government enacted several harsh tax and impressment policies against southern civilians.

134 Warren Clark (1800–1870) wrote this letter to his Democratic son Adin B. Clark (1831–1915).

135 For several days in July 1863, a mostly Irish mob in New York City rioted in opposition to the draft, in the process killing nearly 120 people, including many innocent African Americans who were murdered on the streets.

136 It is unclear who this is.

137 James W. Wall (1820–1872), a Peace Democrat from New Jersey, held a seat in the US Senate for less than two months in early 1863. Earlier in the war he had been arrested for disloyalty.

138 Confederate policy was to kill or enslave black enlisted men (and their white officers), treating them as slaves in insurrection. The Lincoln administration responded by refusing to exchange Confederate prisoners of war if the Confederacy would not recognize all US soldiers.

139 Around the time of the Gettysburg Address, Lincoln contracted a mild form of smallpox known as varioloid.

140 The author of this letter, Charles M. Heaton, was a citizen of South Bend, Ind., who obtained a position with the Land Office (which was located in the Patent Office) through his personal connection with Speaker of the House Schuyler Colfax of Indiana.

141 Salmon P. Chase had two daughters, Kate Chase Sprague, who was a Washington socialite during the war, and Janet ("Nettie").

142 By the time of the presidential election of 1864, nineteen northern states had passed legislation permitting soldiers to vote in the field. Republicans almost universally supported the legislation, while Democrats generally opposed it. Most of the states that refused to give soldiers the franchise, such as Illinois and Indiana, had at least partial Democratic control of the state legislature.

143 We are uncertain of this word, but it appears to be a phonetic spelling of canaller, i.e., laborers who work on a canal. The 100th New York was raised in Buffalo, near the Erie Canal.

144 The Republican Party held its national convention in Baltimore June 7–8, 1864. During the campaign, the Republicans styled themselves the Union Party.

145 Throughout the war Salmon P. Chase used his position as secretary of the treasury to vie for the Republican nomination for president; however, in early March 1864, he formally withdrew from the race after the Ohio legislature overwhelmingly endorsed Lincoln's renomination and reelection.

146 Maj. Gen. Nathaniel P. Banks (1816–1894) was a Democrat-turned-Know Nothing-turned-Republican who had previously served as Speaker of the US House of Representatives and governor of Massachusetts.

147 DeWitt Davis (1833–1905), a lawyer, wrote this to St. Paul attorney Robert Field Crowell.

148 On Tuesday, April 5, 1864, the president and first lady went to Grover's Theatre to hear Friedrich von Flotow's romantic comic opera *Martha; or, The Fair of Richmond* sung by the Arion Society with the Grand Orchestra from New York's Academy of Music. They had gone to Grover's the night before for a performance of Carl Von Weber's *Der Freischütz*.

149 Josephine "Josie" Elizabeth (Bottum) Bunnell (1844–1936) wrote this letter to her sister-in-law, Damaris B. Bunnell (1833–1916) of Dansville, N.Y.. Bunnell's husband was an officer in the 13th New York Infantry.

150 Judge Calvin Gilbert Tilden (1805–1868) of Middlebury, Vt., sent this to Edson Emery (1833–1915) of the 2nd Vermont Infantry.

151 In March, Lincoln appointed Ulysses S. Grant (1822–1885) as lieutenant general, a rank authorized by Congress specifically for him. For the remainder of the war he would travel with the Army of the Potomac in Virginia.

152 John P. Hughes (ca. 1817–1869), a resident of Indiana, went into business as an importer in Hawaii in the 1850s.

153 Here Minturn wrote an underline rather than name the person she was thinking of.

154 Anne (Robinson) Minturn (1827–1917) wrote this to her husband, Lloyd Minturn (1810–1873).

155 Dr. Robert Jefferson Breckinridge (1800–1871) was a Presbyterian minister from Kentucky who supported Lincoln in the election of 1860 against his own nephew, Vice President John C. Breckinridge, the southern Democratic candidate for president.

156 Earlier in the letter Shinn had described signal towers located near the James River.

157 John Brough (1811–1865), a War Democrat, was elected governor of Ohio in 1863, defeating Democrat Clement L. Vallandigham.

158 Typescripts of Fisk's diaries are held at the Library of Congress.

159 Maj. Gen. Ambrose Burnside authorized Pennsylvania coalminers of the 48th Pennsylvania Infantry to dig a tunnel under Confederate lines to blow up their fortifications. The July 30, 1864, attack did not go as planned, and many African American soldiers wound up running into the crater that was created by the explosion, where they were easy targets for the Confederates overhead.

160 It is unclear what cases the writer was referring to in this letter, although two white Union soldiers were executed for desertion on August 5 and 8, 1864, in Virginia.

161 The Cornelius Van Houten Papers are held at the Library of Congress.

162 Confederates led by Brig. Gen. John McCausland burned Chambersburg, Pa., on July 30, 1864, in retaliation for the burning of homes in the Shenandoah Valley by Union soldiers under Maj. Gen. David Hunter.

163 The Democrats held their national convention at Chicago August 29–31, 1864. The Democrats were badly divided between their Peace wing and the more moderate wing of the party that was pro-war but also pro-slavery.

164 On May 31, 1864, the Radical Democrats nominated John C. Fremont as their candidate for president at a convention held in Cleveland. Knowing that Fremont's candidacy would split the Republican vote, party leaders prevailed upon him to withdraw from the race, which he did on September 22. The following day, according to a pre-arranged deal, Montgomery Blair, a conservative in Lincoln's cabinet who was one of Fremont's bitterest political opponents, was relieved of his duties as postmaster general.

165 James Hastings Drennen (1817–1896), a cabinet maker and farmer who had gone from Democrat to Republican, wrote this letter to Capt. James Galbreath Theaker (1830–1910) of the 50th Ohio Infantry.

166 The term "miscegenation" was coined by Democrats during the presidential election of 1864. As a hoax, they printed a pamphlet titled *Miscegenation* that was made to look like it had been written by abolitionists who advocated for interracial marriage. While some abolitionists fell for the trick, Lincoln was not taken in by it.

167 Maj. Gen. Winfield Scott Hancock (1824–1886), a hero of Gettysburg, was the Democratic nominee for president in 1880.

168 The Democratic platform declared the war a "failure," which angered many Union soldiers. Moreover, the war looked less like a failure after Maj. Gen. William T. Sherman captured Atlanta in September 1864.

169 Horatio Seymour (1810–1886), a prominent Democrat and outspoken Lincoln critic, served as governor of New York from 1863 to 1864. He lost his bid for reelection in 1864.

170 In accordance with its state constitution of 1838, Pennsylvania's 1864 law enfranchising soldiers required a 10-cent tax for privates or noncommissioned officers to vote. Commissioned officers had to pay the usual county tax.

171 The recipient of this letter, Hawthorn's niece Susie, lived in Maine. In the Maine gubernatorial election, which had been held on September 12, 1864, incumbent Republican Samuel Cony had won nearly 59 percent of the vote.

172 Henry C. Edgington wrote this letter to his niece, Rhoda Richards.

173 The 1864 New York law that authorized soldiers to vote required soldiers to mail their ballots home to be counted with the "home vote." As a consequence, it is impossible to know how New York soldiers voted in the presidential election. The mail-in voting also had significant fraud.

174 George B. McClellan's Peninsula Campaign came to a disastrous end on July 1, 1862, at the Battle of Malvern Hill. During the battle McClellan boarded the USS *Galena* to inspect areas around Harrison's Landing. Two years later, during the presidential election, Republicans criticized McClellan for being safely aboard the ironclad away from the fighting.

175 Democrats nominated George H. Pendleton (1825–1889), a congressman from Ohio, as McClellan's running mate. The "peace" platform and the nomination of a Peace Democrat for vice president caused many soldiers to vote for Lincoln or abstain from voting in the election.

176 This may be a nautical term referring to the right bow of a ship, a term from the game euchre referring to the jack of the trump suit, or it may simply refer to one who bows or bends.

177 Maj. Gen. Don Carlos Buell (1818–1898) proved to be too hesitant and blundering for Lincoln, who removed him from command of the Army of the Ohio in October 1862. Many at the time believed Buell was disloyal, a charge Ulysses S. Grant vehemently denied.

178 Maj. Gen. Fitz John Porter (1822–1901), a Democrat who had been a close associate of George B. McClellan, was court-martialed in 1863 for misconduct at Second Bull Run. He was dismissed from the service in January 1863.

179 Richard Yates (1815–1873), a Republican and a friend of Lincoln's, served as governor of Illinois from 1861 to 1865.

180 George Eastman (1838–1907), a Quaker from Bucks County, Pa., wrote this letter to his cousin Hugh B. Eastburn (1846–1915) back in New Hope, Pa.

181 Sumner Hill (1838–1878), chief clerk in the Salem Post Office and later a justice of the peace for Essex County, wrote this letter to his brother John.

182 Dr. Peres S. Randall (1803–1867) had served as a surgeon with the 5th (West) Virginia Infantry and the 14th Kentucky Mounted Infantry. Service records indicate he was discharged on September 20, 1864.

183 Friedrich Hassaurek (1831–1885), an Austrian immigrant who had taken part in the failed German Revolutions of 1848, became a lawyer, journalist, and Republican orator in Cincinnati, Ohio.

184 Levi Jay Brown (1838–1883) sent this letter to his sister Ellen A. Brown (1846–1928) back home in Freedom, Portage County, Ohio.

185 Lincoln delivered his fourth annual message to Congress on December 6, 1864. Unlike the State of the Union speech today, which is delivered in person by the president, Lincoln sent a printed message to Congress, where it was read by the clerk of the House of Representatives.

186 Thomas W. Hendee (1829–1867), a native of Portsmouth, N.H., made his living as a purchaser and outfitter of steamships for Stearns, Hobart & Co.—a firm that operated the Bombay and Bengal Steamship Company in India. Hendee was based in England but made frequent trips to India to oversee operations in Bombay and Calcutta.

187 John Deering Jr. (1842–1915) of Saco, Maine, was a student at Bowdoin College in 1860, but he enlisted as a private in the 13th Maine Infantry in December 1861 and served until August 16, 1862. He had to leave due to a disability, no doubt related to an accident while working as a clerk in the partially constructed custom office at New Orleans. According to his biographical sketch in a family history, he fell through a scuttle in the custom house roof and dropped 30 feet but somehow managed to survive the fall. Following his discharge, he worked for a time in the Treasury Department and earned a degree from the Columbia College Law School in 1866. His obituary in the *Lewiston Sun* claims that he "saw the assassination of President Lincoln and heard the last speech by the President, made from a window of the White House three days before he was shot." This letter is in the Stacy Family Papers, Virginia Museum of History and Culture, Richmond, Va.

188 On February 3, 1865, Lincoln and Seward met with Confederate commissioners, including Vice President Alexander H. Stephens, to discuss terms of peace. During this four-hour meeting aboard the *River Queen*, anchored near Fort Monroe in Hampton Roads, Va., Lincoln insisted that Confederates must lay down their arms and accept federal authority. He also maintained that "slavery must be abolished," although he appears to have still contemplated some form of compensation for slaveholders (his cabinet rejected this idea two days later). Nothing came of this meeting because the Confederates were not yet willing to surrender.

189 Rev. Arthur B. Bradford (1810–1899) was an abolitionist and Presbyterian minister. The letter is held in the Cameron Papers at the Library of Congress.

190 The "colors" refers to the unit's flag.

191 Frances Anne (Sutton) Doswell (1837–1903) kept a diary of the fall of Richmond from April 2 to April 26, 1865. Her husband, Thomas Walker Doswell (1823–1890), was a soldier in the Confederate army. The diary is in the Doswell Family Papers, Virginia Museum of History and Culture, Richmond, Va.

192 William H. Hanna, an attorney and old acquaintance of Lincoln's, sent this letter to Lincoln's friend and self-appointed bodyguard, Ward Hill Lamon. It is held in Lamon's papers at the Huntington Library in San Marino, Calif.

193 David Spielman (born 1800), a carpenter, wrote this letter to his daughter Mary Jane (Spielman) Miller (1826–1883). He had two sons serving in the Union army.

194 On April 13, Oakes Smith was invited to address a meeting in her community on April 14 to celebrate the end of the war.

195 Lincoln was shot just after 10 p.m. at Ford's Theatre in Washington, DC.

196 Elizabeth Oakes Smith (1806–1893) was a prominent first wave feminist writer and public speaker whose life was derailed by the arrest of her son Appleton Oaksmith for slave trading in 1861. Although she was a reformer with sympathies for abolitionism, Oakes Smith was a Democrat who grew to loathe the Lincoln administration—especially Secretary of State Seward—during the war. Elizabeth Oakes Smith Papers, Albert and Shirley Small Special Collections Library, University of Virginia, Charlottesville, Va.

197 In the box with Lincoln were Mary as well as an engaged couple, Maj. Henry Rathbone and Clara Harris, the daughter of a US senator.

198 Oakes Smith Papers, University of Virginia.

199 The Old Capitol Prison, which was located on the current site of the US Supreme Court, served as the Capitol Building from 1815 to 1819, after the British burned the US Capitol during the War of 1812. During the Civil War it housed Confederate prisoners of war as well as spies and political prisoners.

200 Sarah Goodrich, a devout Methodist, sent this letter to her sister Augusta Goodrich Griffing—William J. Griffing's great-great-grandmother. The original letter is held at the Kansas Historical Society in Topeka.

201 Southerners often referred to Union soldiers as "blue bellies."

202 John Wilkes Booth (1838–1865) evaded capture for 12 days before Union troops finally caught up with him in Port Royal, Va.

203 Clements appears to have written "treacherous" a second time, but he almost certainly meant "traitorous."

204 William H. Seward was in bed recuperating from a carriage accident when John Wilkes Booth's co-conspirator Lewis Powell (a.k.a. Payne) forced himself into Seward's bedroom and tried to stab him to death. Powell also attacked Seward's sons Frederick and Augustus, his daughter Fanny, and a soldier who was at the home as a guard.

205 Benjamin Willson Briggs (born 1842), an employee of the Assessor's Office of the US Internal Revenue Service, 8th Illinois District, wrote this letter to his older sister Rhoda Sophia Briggs (1840–1921). This letter is courtesy of the Senft family.

206 The Knights of the Golden Circle (KGC) and Sons of Liberty (mentioned in a May 1865 letter) were Democratic secret societies suspected of wanting to aid the Confederacy and overthrow the Union from within. While the Sons and the KGC were particularly strong in the Midwest, historians disagree over whether they posed a real threat to the Union or were more of a paper tiger.

207 Laura J. Morgan (1845–1928) wrote this to her beau, Lt. William Henry Thurston (1838–1924) of the 1st Pennsylvania Light Artillery.

208 Sophia Morton (Williams) Harris (1804–1880) wrote this to her younger sister, Mary (Williams) Brayman (1816–1886) of Springfield, Ill. Mary's husband, Mason Brayman (1813–1895), was a prominent lawyer and politician in Springfield who rented the Lincoln home during Lincoln's term in Congress in the late 1840s.

209 Helen Augusta "Nellie" Barnard wrote this letter to her future husband, Sgt. James Kipp Underhill (1837–1905) of the 13th New York Heavy Artillery.

210 Some abolitionists and Radical Republicans rejoiced when Lincoln was assassinated because they expected Andrew Johnson to be much harsher toward the South; they would be sorely disappointed.

211 Samuel Musser Fry Jr. (1845–1924), a miller in Lancaster County, Pa., wrote this letter to his boyhood friend William Jackson Fraser (1835–1910) of the 195th Pennsylvania Infantry.

212 Confederate general Joseph E. Johnston surrendered to William T. Sherman at Bennett Place, N.C., on April 26, 1865. Grant was not present at the surrender.

213 Booth had been born in the slave state of Maryland, but Petrie may be considering him a northern man because Maryland remained in the Union.

214 Dr. John Kingree France (1825–1887) was a native of Roanoke, Va., who moved to Ohio and Kansas before settling in California in 1864. He wrote this letter to his younger brother, Charles Beeson France (1835–1895), in Denver.

215 Booth was shot and killed in a barn in Port Royal, Va., on April 26, 1865. Contrary to this report, he is buried in an unmarked grave in his family plot at Green Mount Cemetery in Baltimore.

216 Joseph H. Prime (1841–1911), a native of Dover, N.H., served as corporal in the 13th New Hampshire Infantry before becoming an officer in the 7th US Colored Infantry. This letter, which was written to Prime's wife, Hannah (Snell) Prime (1841–1920), is courtesy of Jim Doncaster.

217 Mary Louise Meeker (1842–1903) wrote this to Capt. Joseph Burdin (1839–1904) of the 50th New York Engineers, whom she would marry in November 1865.

218 Frederick Newton Barger (1813–1902), a mechanic and gunsmith, wrote this to his acquaintance Joseph Mast Maitland (1838–1918) of the 95th Ohio Infantry.

219 This letter is held in the Hood Family Papers, Abraham Lincoln Presidential Library and Museum, Springfield, Ill.

220 William Thomas Applegate (1831–1904) had served as an officer in the 28th Kentucky Infantry before resigning his commission in November 1862. It is not clear why he was in Washington, DC, at this time.

221 Emma E. Davis (1842–1927) of Strafford County, N.H., worked as a store clerk in Boston during the last year or two of the Civil War. She wrote this to her cousin William Sydney Gray (1836–1907) of the 12th New Hampshire Infantry.

222 George W. Fraser (1841–1912) had previously served in the 195th Pennsylvania Infantry (see his letter of July 29, 1864).

223 Here Farrington quoted an account of the battle from volume 1 of G. G. Benedict's *Vermont in the Civil War* (1886), p. 489.

224 George Edwin Farrington (1842–1913) of Elgin, Ill., had served in the 3rd Vermont Infantry during the war. He wrote this to John E. Boos (1879–1974) of Albany, N.Y., a collector of personal recollections related to Lincoln and the Civil War.

225 At age 91, William Critchley (1836–1932) recounted meeting Lincoln at City Point, Va., in March 1865, while serving as the band leader of the 3rd Brigade, 3rd Division, 24th Army Corps. This letter was also written to John E. Boos.

Index

About the Editors

Jonathan W. White is professor of American Studies at Christopher Newport University. He is the prize-winning author or editor of 18 books, including his first children's book, *My Day with Abe Lincoln.* He serves as vice chair of The Lincoln Forum, on the boards of directors of the Abraham Lincoln Association and the Abraham Lincoln Institute, and on the Ford's Theatre Advisory Council. In 2023 he won the Gilder Lehrman Lincoln Prize for *A House Built by Slaves: African American Visitors to the Lincoln White House.*

With an undergraduate degree from Kansas State University and an MS in radiation physics from Purdue University, **William J. Griffing** enjoyed a successful 30-year career in the environment, safety, and health field. He held positions at the Department of Labor and the Department of Energy before serving as the ES&H director at both the National Renewable Energy Laboratory and the Fermi National Accelerator Laboratory. Since retiring, he has dedicated a significant amount of his time to preserving American history, with a particular focus on the Civil War era.